knit

knit

Designs by
Diana Crossing, Amanda Ducker,
Sarah Durrant, Janine Flew,
Liz Gemmell, Amanda McKittrick,
Stephanie J. Milne, Jane Slicer-Smith,
Nancy Tyack, and Nicola Wilkins

THUNDER BAY
P·R·E·S·S
San Diego, California

contents

techniques

projects

Introduction

The past few seasons have seen a revival in the art of hand knitting. Many new knitters are discovering the pleasures and therapeutic benefits of this traditional craft. In an increasingly frenetic, mechanized, technology-driven world, many people are attracted to pursuits that are just the opposite. Many knitters find that their craft becomes an opportunity for some time out; a chance to create, reflect and relax. The meditative rhythm of knitting provides a counterpoint to the busy pace of everyday life and an opportunity to connect with tradition and your own creativity.

Although commercially knitted garments are often much cheaper than those you knit yourself, there is no comparison in quality, or in the satisfaction of having made a unique garment. Think of knitting as an investment; the time and money you spend are well recompensed with a beautiful hand-knitted item that you can use, admire and love for years to come. A sweater or rug seems all the more cozy if you have knitted it yourself, or if it has been knitted for you by a loved one.

Although knitting isn't reliant on technology, there are certain aspects of technology that can make knitting simpler and more accessible. Many knitters' websites and chat rooms exist; these can be a valuable source of advice, help and free patterns. Internet mail order is a boon for finding yarns — including elusive, speciality and hand-spun yarns that may be difficult to find in stores — and for knitters in isolated places.

Many keen knitters have several projects on the go at the one time: perhaps a simple item such as a garter-stitch scarf to knit in front of the television; a plain sweater that requires a little more attention; and a challenge knit, such as an intricate lace or Aran item, that requires patience, concentration and preferably solitude.

This book gives the basic techniques needed to make and finish a garment, as well as 24 original patterns. These range from easy items suitable for beginners to advanced knits requiring both skill and patience. Don't be daunted if you are a novice knitter. A ball of yarn and a pair of knitting needles are all you require to start knitting. You don't necessarily need a lot of skill or time; simple knits in chunky, quick-to-work yarns can be just as satisfying to make as a complex pattern. As your skills advance and you gain confidence, you can expand your collection of equipment and experiment with different yarns and stitch patterns.

braided scarf Three strands of knitted fabric in a chunky velvet-look yarn are braided together.

A brief history of knitting

The origins of knitting are obscure. Fabrics of similar appearance to knitting, but made using a different technique, date back to the fifth century BC. The oldest surviving pieces of true knitting are from Egypt and can be roughly dated to between 1000 and 1400 AD. The first references to true knitting in Europe are from the early 14th century. The first knitting trade guild was established in Paris in 1527, and the trade remained male dominated for centuries to come.

Britain had a thriving cottage industry in knitting, especially of stockings, in the 14th and 15th centuries. On various groups of Scottish islands in the 17th and 18th centuries, whole families were involved in the making of knitted garments. Distinctive regional variations in knitting styles developed, among them fair isle patterns and shetland lace in Scotland, and richly cabled and textured Aran designs in Ireland. Knitted sweaters were essential to the fishing communities of these islands, as the natural oils in the wool provided some degree of weather proofing. The designs were sometimes specific to a particular family, enabling the remains of lost seamen to be identified by the sweater they were wearing.

The first knitting machine, designed to make stockings, was invented in Nottingham, England, in 1589 by William Lee, a clergyman. Later, the industrial revolution made it possible to spin yarn of uniform consistency and also enabled the mass production of knitted cloth. Women came to be employed in factories rather than at home spinning and knitting their own garments; this, and the availability of cheaper mass-produced knitted goods, led to a decline in hand knitting. The skill was now practiced mainly by women, and as a hobby, not a way of life.

In more recent times, knitting's popularity has fluctuated. In the 1940s, wartime austerity made it a necessity; in the 1950s and 60s, it was fashionable again; and by the 1980s, it had declined worldwide.

However, since the turn of this century, knitting has been on the rise again. Technology and industry, the very factors that contributed to its earlier decline, are now partly responsible for its renewed popularity; the multitude of fancy, exotic, multicolored, and highly textured yarns that are now manufactured have attracted many new knitters to the pleasures of this traditional yet timeless craft.

miter throw A mixture of plain and novelty yarns are combined in this rug.

smooth yarns in wool or wool blends Clockwise from top: plain DK pure wool; plain DK pure wool; DK tweed pure wool; worsted/Aran weight pure wool; flecked DK pure wool; (center) variegated acrylic/wool mix.

Yarns

The choice of yarn is most important. Every type of yarn has distinct properties; different yarns knitted to the same pattern can produce vastly different effects, so you need to match the yarn to the project. For example, for a hard-wearing sweater that can be machine washed, a specially treated wool is the best choice. A baby's garment is better made in cotton, which can stand up to repeated washing and is also cool, so the baby won't overheat.

If your local craft or specialist yarn store doesn't stock the yarn you want, or can't order it in for you, internet mail order is a convenient way of finding and ordering yarns that might otherwise be unobtainable. The shipping fees are generally modest, and it's worth the extra expense to get just the right yarn.

Knitting is usually done with commercial yarns, but any continuous piece of material can be knitted, including strips of plastic or fabric (whether knitted or woven), ribbon, tape and wire.

Yarn types

yarns in other fibers and finishes Clockwise from top: Mohair; slubby pure wool; wool/silk/angora mix; variegated bouclé mohair; alpaca/silk/polyamide mix.

When choosing yarn, you need to consider its content and thickness (or ply) and how the manufacturer has treated the fiber. Yarns may be natural, synthetic or a mixture of both. Natural yarns are obtained either from animals or plants. Yarns of animal origin include wool, from sheep; cashmere and mohair, from goats; angora, from angora rabbits; and alpaca, from a relative of the llama. Plant-derived yarns include cotton, linen and hemp. Synthetic yarns, such as acrylic, polyester and nylon, are often mixed with natural yarns to improve their texture and performance.

Yarns can also be treated and spun to make them hairier, heavier, denser, more twisted, fluffier, flatter or knobblier. Some ways in which manufacturers treat yarns to change their intrinsic characteristics are by giving a shrink-resist treatment to wool to make it machine washable, and mercerizing cotton to give it a luster.

Some terms used to describe yarn (such as silk, cotton, cashmere) refer to the yarn's content; others (such as Aran, tweed, bouclé) to its texture, appearance and/or thickness.

Smooth, plain yarns are best for fancy patterns such as cables and lace, as these yarns enable the beauty and intricacy of the stitches to be easily seen. Fashion or novelty yarns are best used with simple garter stitch or stocking stitch designs; the lovely details of more complicated patterns will be lost in these busy yarns.

When starting out, you may be tempted by the intriguing textures, bright color mixtures, or sensual feel of novelty yarns, but it's best to practie on smooth, plain yarns, which are easiest to knit with. Choose pale or mid-toned yarns; these show stitch details better than dark yarns, which is especially useful if you're practicing more complicated stitch textures or patterns.

Reading a yarn band

On the paper band around the ball of yarn is printed useful information such as the manufacturer and composition of the yarn, the recommended needle size to use, the recommended gauge that the yarn should knit up to, the weight of the ball, care instructions, and the shade and dye lot. All balls for the same garment should come from the same dye lot. Different dye lots can vary in tone; a variation that is undetectable between individual balls can be quite noticeable in the finished garment. If you are forced to mix dye lots, you can make the transition between the two less obvious by alternating two rows of one dye lot with two rows of the other throughout the garment.

novelty yarns Clockwise from top: hairy yarn in acrylic–polyamide mix; chunky velvet-look yarn in exoline; tufted yarn in polyester–polyamide mix; velvet ribbon yarn in nylon–acrylic mix; silky-look 'eyelash' yarn in polyester.

Yarn weights

Yarns come in many thicknesses, from threadlike yarns used for traditional lace to super-bulky yarns that knit up thickly (and gratifyingly quickly). Not all countries use the same terms for types and weights of yarn. Also, some weights of yarn are very popular in some countries and little used in others. The following table lists some of the most popular weights of yarn and their names in different parts of the world, and how many stitches they yield per 4 inches when knitted on the recommended needle size.

International yarn equivalents (note that figures given are approximate and will vary between manufacturers)

U.S.	UK and Canada	Australia/NZ	Gauge per 10 cm (4 in)	Needle
Sport/Baby	Baby	5-ply	24 sts	3.75 mm (US 5/UK 9)
Double knitting (DK)	Double knitting (DK)	8-ply	22 sts	4 mm (US 6/UK 8)
Worsted weight	Aran	10-ply	18–20 sts	5 mm (US 8/UK 6)
Chunky	Chunky	12-ply	14–18 sts	5 or 5.5 mm (US 8 or 9/UK 6 or 5)
Bulky	Bulky	12–14 ply	9–12 sts	8 mm (US 11/UK 0) or up

Equipment

Knitting needles

Knitting needles may be either straight (two or more separate needles) or circular (two needles joined by a length of round plastic or nylon). Needles may be made from various materials, including aluminum, wood, bamboo and plastic.

A piece of knitted fabric can be made either flat or in the round. For example, if making a sweater using flat knitting, the back and front pieces are made separately then joined up the sides. If making a sweater in the round, all the stitches for both the back and the front are cast on at the same time and the body of the sweater is knitted in one piece, in what is effectively a spiral. This eliminates side seams. To do flat knitting, you can use either straight or circular needles; for circular knitting, you will need circular needles and/or a set of double-pointed needles.

Circular needles come in various lengths; if knitting in the round, choose a length that is shorter than the circumference of the piece you are knitting. For example, you cannot knit a piece with a 20 inch circumference on 24 inch needles, as the knitting will be stretched.

Circular needles are particularly useful when knitting large items, such as shawls or rugs; the length of the needle easily accommodates a large numbers of stitches, and the weight of the garment stays centered over your lap rather than awkwardly weighing down one end of the needle, as is the case with straight needles.

Double-pointed needles come in sets of four or five needles about 8 inches in length. The stitches are cast on as normal then divided roughly equally between three or four needles. The last needle in the set is then used to knit off the stitches. Double-pointed needles are useful when knitting parts of garments that may be too narrow for circular needles, such as the collars of sweaters.

Cable needles are short needles used to hold stitches while making a cable. They may be straight, or kinked in the middle to prevent the stitches from slipping off.

Needle size conversion chart

Metric (mm)	U.S.	UK/Canada
2	0	14
2.25	1	13
2.75	2	12
3	–	11
3.25	3	10
3.5	4	–
3.75	5	9
4	6	8
4.5	7	7
5	8	6
5.5	9	5
6	10	4
6.5	10½	3
7	–	2
7.5	–	1
8	11	0
9	13	00
10	15	000
12	17	–
15–16	19	–
19	35	–
25	50	–

Needle sizes

There is no universal guide for knitting needle sizes; they are expressed differently from country to country. Sizes many also vary slightly from one manufacturer to the next. The patterns in this book give U.S. needle sizes. If you need to convert, see the chart at left.

Accessories

The following handy tools may be purchased at craft or yarn stores, or improvised.

Crochet hooks These are useful for picking up dropped stitches or for binding off. The crochet hook does not have to be the same size as the needle you are using for the work; it can be a little smaller or larger without affecting the fabric too much.

Metal ruler Used for checking gauge; more accurate than a cloth tape measure.

Needle gauge Used for checking the size of knitting needles; some also have metric and imperial measurements marked on the sides, for measuring gauge squares.

Pins For marking out gauge squares, pinning garments into shape before blocking or pressing, and pinning knitted pieces together before sewing up.

Row counter A cylindrical gadget that fits on the end of the needle; it has numbered tumblers that can be turned at the end of each row to record how many rows you have done. Useful, but not essential; you can improvise with pen and paper.

Stitch holders Made of metal and resembling large safety pins, these come in various sizes and are used to hold stitches that will be picked up again later, for example at a neck edge. For small numbers of stitches, you can improvise with safety pins.

Stitch markers Small plastic rings slipped onto the needle to mark the start of a pattern repeat or, in circular knitting, the start of a row; you can improvise with small loops of contrasting yarn (see at right).

Tape measure For measuring garment pieces.

Wool needle For sewing up seams and darning in ends of yarn on finished pieces; it should have a blunt end so as not to split the strands of yarn.

Using stitch markers

Commercially produced stitch markers are small plastic rings of varying diameters, to fit different-sized needles (see the center photograph below). Alternatively, you can make your own; using short lengths of contrast-colored yarn, make a small slipknot in each and slip one loop onto the needle where required. As you come to each marker on successive rows, simply slip it off the left needle and onto the right.

When casting on a lot of stitches, you may find it useful to put a marker after every 20 stitches to assist in counting.

Markers can also help you keep track of pattern repeats, for example in lace, Aran or other complex patterns. Place a marker at the start of each pattern repeat; then, if you make a mistake, it will be easier to trace where it occurred.

If working in the round on circular or double-pointed needles, slip on a marker to show where each new round begins.

needles (from top right) Double-pointed, straight, circular, and cable needles (straight and kinked).

accessories (from top left) Wool needle, crochet hook, stitch markers, row counter, pins.

accessories (from top) Tape measure, ruler; needle gauge, safety pin, stitch holders, scissors.

Casting on

Casting on is the term given to making the first row of stitches; these form the foundation of your knitting. There are several methods of casting on. The following are two of the most versatile. The golden rule of casting on is to do so loosely; even if you think your cast-on is too loose, it probably isn't.

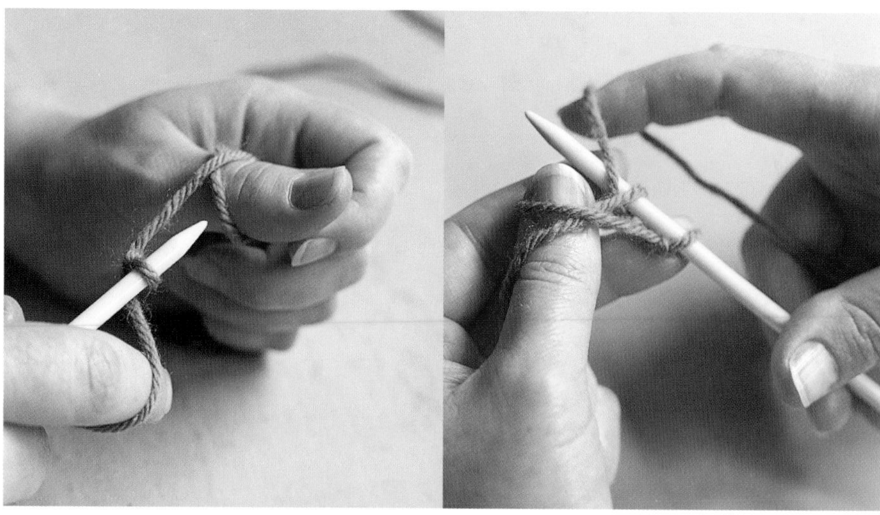

step four Insert the point of the right needle into the loop around your thumb.

step five Wrap the ball end of yarn around the needle.

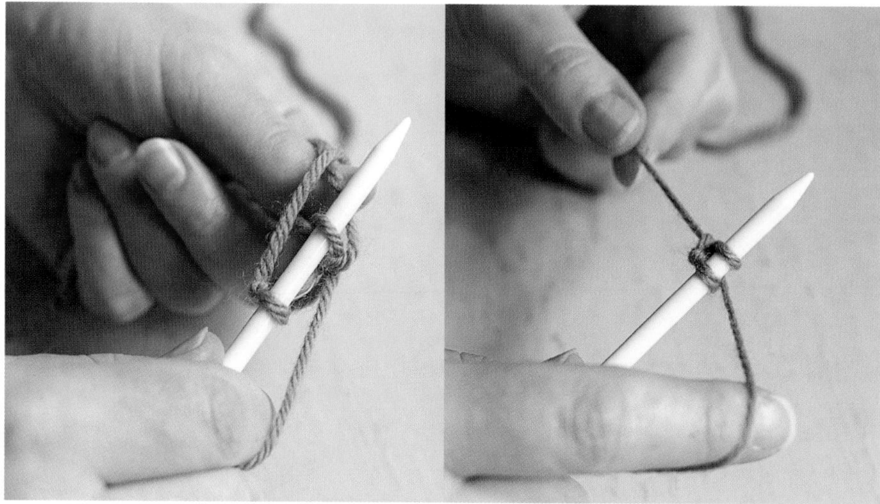

step five continued Pull the ball end of yarn through the thumb loop to make a stitch.

step six Pull on the ball end of the yarn until the loop is firm but not tight.

Thumb method

This gives a very flexible edge and is especially good for rib edges of garments and for garter stitch fabric.

1 Start with a length of yarn measuring a little more than three times the width of the edge to be cast on. Make a slipknot (see opposite) at this point.

2 Transfer the slipknot to a knitting needle. Draw it up until it is close to the needle, but not tight; you should be able to easily insert a second needle into the loop.

3 With the tail end of the yarn, make a clockwise loop around your thumb.

4 Insert the point of the right needle from front to back into the thumb loop.

5 Wrap the ball end of yarn around the needle and pull this loop through the thumb loop. You have now cast on a stitch.

6 Pull on the ball end of yarn until the stitch is firm, but not tight; you should be able to easily insert a second needle into the loop.

7 Repeat Steps 3–6 until you have cast on the required number of stitches. (Remember that the loop of the slipknot counts as one stitch.)

Cable method

Also known as the two-needle method, this gives a smooth edge and is particularly compatible with stocking stitch. It is not as flexible as the thumb method, so tension it loosely if it is to become the bottom, neck or sleeve edge of a garment.

1 Leaving a tail of yarn about 6 inches long, make a slipknot on the left needle.

2 Holding the other needle in your right hand, insert its point from left to right into the loop of the slipknot.

3 Hook the yarn around the tip of the right-hand needle and pull it through the loop of the slipknot.

4 Put the loop just made onto the left-hand needle. You have now cast on a stitch. *Gently* pull the ball end of the yarn to secure the loop. If a needle will not pass easily through the loop with almost no resistance, the loop is too tight.

5 Insert the right-hand needle between the previous loop and the loop you just made. Hook the yarn around the tip of the right-hand needle and draw it through. Place the loop just made onto the left-hand needle and gently tighten.

6 Repeat Step 5 until you have the required number of stitches. (The slip loop counts as one stitch.)

Making a slipknot

Make a loop in a piece of yarn. Bring the yarn up from back to front through the loop and pull to tighten. You have now made a slipknot. Place the loop on the knitting needle or crochet hook. You can now begin casting on or making a crochet chain. Remember that the loop of the slipknot counts as the first cast-on or chain stitch.

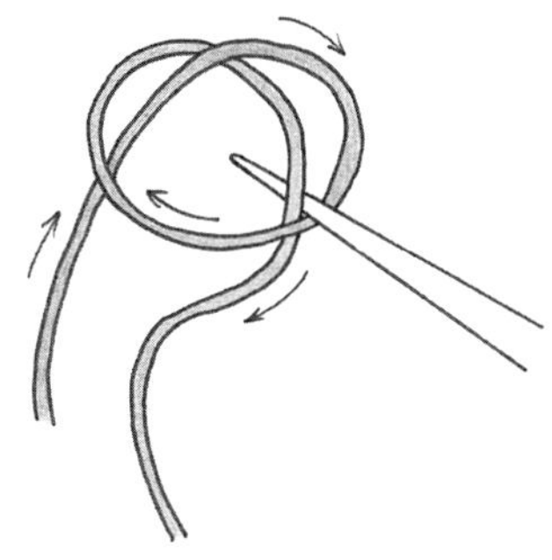

step two Insert the point of the right needle into the loop of the slipknot.

step three Hook the yarn around the tip of the right needle and pull the yarn through.

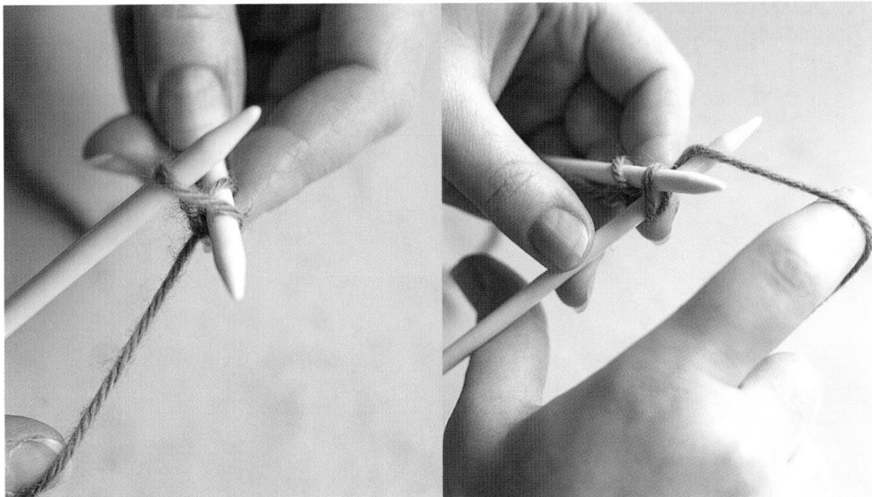

step four Put the loop just made onto the left needle and gently tighten.

step five Insert the tip of the right needle between the two loops and draw the yarn through.

The basic stitches

Knitting has just two basic stitches, the knit stitch and the purl stitch. Many different stitch patterns, including textures, cables, twists, bobbles, and ribs, can be made from these alone.

Garter stitch

If you knit every row, the resulting fabric is known as garter stitch (above). It has a ridged appearance, and both sides of the fabric are identical. The fabric lies flat, without curling up at the edges.

Hint

If you look closely at the stitches on a knitting needle, you will see that they do not lie at right angles to the needle. Instead, the front 'leg' of the stitch lies slightly to the right and the back leg slightly to the left. Keep this in mind, especially if knitting a stitch that you have picked up; if you knit into the back (left leg) rather than the front (right leg) of the stitch, you will twist the stitch and it will look different to all the other stitches in the row.

The knit stitch

1 Insert the point of the right needle from left to right through the front of the first stitch on the left needle.

2 Wrap the yarn around the tip of the right needle.

3 With the tip of the right needle, draw the yarn through the stitch on the left needle.

4 Slip the original stitch off the left needle. You have now made a knit stitch.

5 Repeat Steps 1–4 until you reach the end of the row. To start the next row, you need to turn to the work. To do this, transfer the needle in your right hand, with the work on it, to the left hand; the empty needle is held in the right hand. You are now ready to begin knitting the second row.

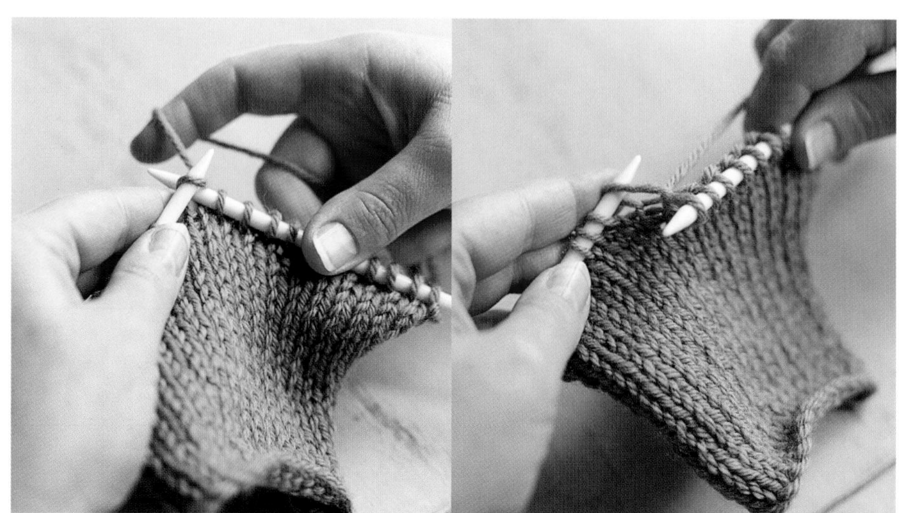

step one Insert the point of the right needle through the stitch on the left needle.

step three With the tip of the right needle, draw the yarn through the stitch on the left needle.

The purl stitch

The purl stitch is, in effect, the reverse of the knit stitch.

1 Insert the point of the right needle from right to left into the front of the first stitch on the left needle.

2 Wrap the yarn around the tip of the right needle.

3 With the tip of the right needle, draw the yarn through the stitch on the left needle.

4 Slip the original stitch off the left needle. You have now made a purl stitch.

5 Repeat Steps 1–4 until you reach the end of the row, then turn the work and begin the next row.

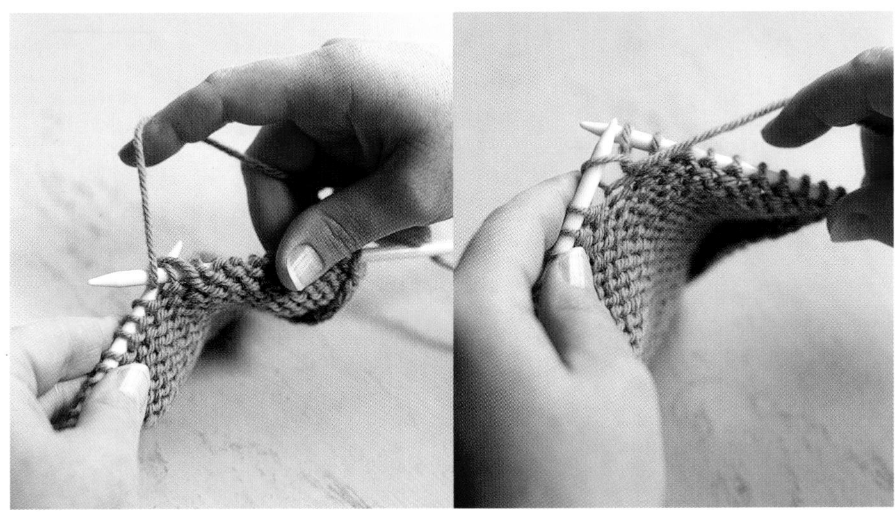

step two Wrap the yarn around the tip of the right needle.

step three With the tip of the right needle, draw the yarn through the stitch on the left needle.

Stockinette

If you knit and purl alternate rows, the resulting fabric is known as stockinette. One side of the fabric is smooth, with stitches looking like little Vs. The other side is knobbly and looks similar to garter stitch. Usually the smooth side is used as the right side. If the knobbly side is used, the fabric is known as reverse stockinette. The difference in using reverse stockinette rather than garter stitch when you want a knobbly look on the right side is that reverse stockinette fabric is thinner than garter stitch fabric, giving a less bulky garment.

If you purl every row, you get garter stitch, but as purl stitch is slower to make than knit stitch, there is no advantage to making a garter-stitch fabric by purling.

Increasing

Increasing and decreasing are ways of shaping the fabric. There are several methods of increasing; the following are two of the most useful. Increasing is usually, but not always, done on a right-side row. It may be done at the edge or in the body of the piece of knitted fabric.

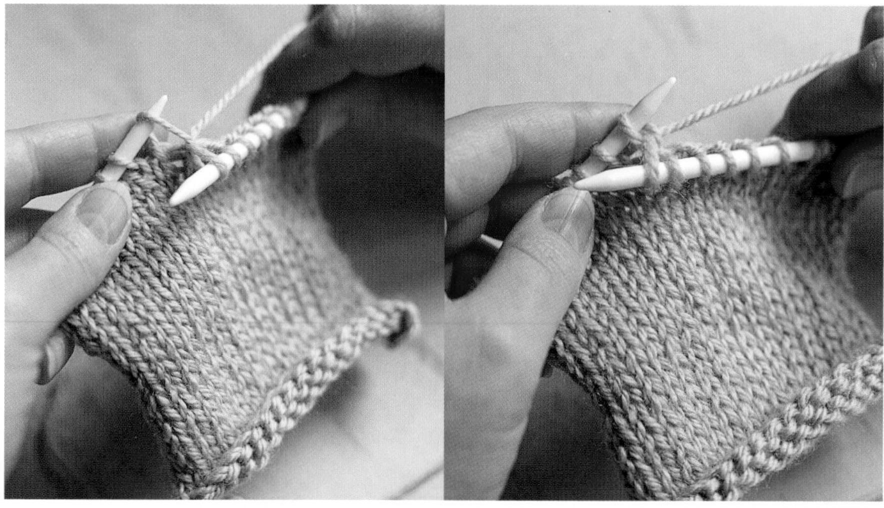

knit fabric, step one Knit a stitch as usual, but do not slip the stitch off the left needle.

knit fabric, step two Knit into back of same stitch, then slip the stitch off the left needle.

purl fabric, step one Purl a stitch as usual, but do not slip the stitch off the left needle.

purl fabric, step two Purl into back of same stitch, then slip the stitch off the left needle.

Working into the back and front of a stitch (inc)

Working into both the back and front of the same stitch produces a neat but slightly visible increase. This increase can be done on either knit or purl fabric. Both versions are shown here. This increase is usually abbreviated simply as inc, but you may also see it as kfb (knit into front and back) or pfb (purl into front and back).

INC ON KNIT FABRIC

1 Knit a stitch as usual, but do not slip the stitch off the left needle.

2 Insert the tip of the right needle into the back of the same stitch, from front to back and right to left. (You may need to wriggle the needle about a little to enlarge the loop, especially if your gauge is tight.) Knit the stitch, then slip the stitch off the left needle. You have now made an extra knit stitch.

INC ON PURL FABRIC

1 Purl a stitch as usual, but do not slip the stitch off the left needle.

2 Insert the tip of the right needle into the back of the same stitch, from back to front and left to right. Knit the stitch, then slip the stitch off the left needle. You have now made an extra purl stitch.

Making a stitch (M1)

Another method of increasing is by working into the running stitch — that is, the thread that lies between two stitches. Working into the back of the stitch (rather than the front, as is usual) twists the stitch and prevents a hole from forming, making the increase almost invisible. This is particularly useful if you need to increase in the body of the garment. This increase is usually abbreviated as M1 (make a stitch), and can be done on either knit or purl fabric; both versions are shown here.

M1 ON KNIT FABRIC

1 With the tip of the left needle, pick up the loop that lies between the first stitch on that needle and the first stitch on the right needle. Make sure that the front of the loop slopes to the right.

2 Knit into the back of the loop. You have now made an extra knit stitch.

M1 ON PURL FABRIC

1 With the tip of the left needle, pick up the loop that lies between the first stitch on that needle and the first stitch on the right needle. Make sure that the front of the loop slopes to the right.

2 Purl into the back of the loop. You have now made an extra purl stitch.

knit fabric, step one With tip of left needle, pick up the loop lying between the two stitches.

knit fabric, step two Knit into the back of the loop that you have just picked up.

purl fabric, step one With tip of left needle, pick up the loop lying between the two stitches.

purl fabric, step two Purl into the back of the loop that you have just picked up.

Decreasing

By working one or more stitches together, thus decreasing the number of stitches in a row, you can shape a knitted piece. Decreasing may be done at either the edge or in the body of the knitting, and on both knit and purl fabric.

Hints

The number of normal rows worked between one decrease row and the next determines how steep the angle of the decrease will be. Decreasing every row produces a steep angle; decreasing less often, for example every fourth or sixth row, produces a shallower angle.

Perfecting your decreases

The most rudimentary decrease is made by working together the first or last two stitches in a row. However, a much neater look is achieved by making 'fully fashioned' decreases; these are worked a consistent number of stitches (usually two or three) in from each end of the knitting.

To make the decreases at each end mirror each other, you will need to make one of them slope to the right and the other to the left. To make a right-sloping decrease, work two stitches together through the front of the stitch as explained at right. To make a left-sloping decrease, work two stitches together through the back of the stitch.

Working in this way emphasizes the way the knitting is shaped, or 'fashioned'. It results in a decorative effect at the decreased edge, and will add a professional touch to your knitting.

KNITTING TWO STITCHES TOGETHER (ABBREVIATED AS K2TOG)

Insert the tip of the right needle into the first two stitches on the left needle, from left to right and front to back as normal. Pass the yarn around the right needle and knit a stitch, slipping both original stitches off the left needle. You have now decreased by one stitch. (It is usual to decrease by one stitch at a time, but sometimes you may be instructed to k3tog, thus decreasing two stitches.)

PURLING TWO STITCHES TOGETHER (ABBREVIATED AS P2TOG)

Insert the tip of the right needle into the first two stitches on the left needle, from right to left and back to front as normal. Pass the yarn around the right needle and purl a stitch, slipping both original stitches off the left needle. You have now decreased by one stitch. (It is usual to decrease by one stitch at a time, but sometimes you may be instructed to p3tog, thus decreasing two stitches.)

k2tog Two stitches are knitted together, then the original stitch is slipped off the left needle.

p2tog Two stitches are purled together, then the original stitch is slipped off the left needle.

Picking up stitches along edge

An edging, border or collar can be added to the main piece of knitting by picking up stitches from a cast-on, bound-off or side edge. This can be done with a knitting needle or a crochet hook. In some patterns, you may see this technique referred to as 'pick up and knit' or 'knit up'.

1 With right side of work facing, insert the tip of the right needle (or the crochet hook) into the edge of the knitting. Work one stitch in from the edge on a side or shaped edge, or under both loops of a cast-on or bound-off edge.

2 Draw through a loop of yarn; you have now picked up a stitch.

Repeat Steps 1–2 until you have picked up the required number of stitches.

If using a crochet hook, pick up as many stitches as will comfortably fit along the length of the hook, then slip these off the end of the crochet hook onto a knitting needle of the specified size. Repeat this process until you have picked up the required number of stitches.

When picking up along a slanting bound-off edge (for example a V-neck edge), you will need to insert the needle into the stitches one row below the decrease, not between the stitches, as this may form a hole. Always make sure the stitches are evenly spaced along the edge.

step one Insert the tip of the right needle from front to back into the edge of the work.

step two Draw through a loop of yarn; you have now picked up (or knitted up) a stitch.

Crochet hook method, step one Insert hook into edge of fabric and draw a loop through.

Crochet hook method, step two Transfer picked-up stitches from hook to knitting needle.

Picking up dropped stitches

Even the best knitter will occasionally drop a stitch or make it incorrectly. The mistake can easily be rectified using the following methods. A dropped or incorrectly made stitch can be traced back and fixed in this manner for several rows, if need be.

Hint

You may not notice that you have dropped a stitch until several rows after it has occurred, when you stop to look at your work or to count stitches. A dropped stitch will form a ladder in the fabric, and should be stopped as soon as possible, or it will unwind further down the work.

If you notice a dropped stitch but are in the middle of a complicated pattern that you don't want to lose track of, put a safety pin through the dropped stitch to keep it from unraveling further, then come back to it once you have finished the row you are on.

To pick up a dropped stitch on stockinette fabric, with right side facing you, insert a crochet hook into the dropped stitch from the front. Pick up the first horizontal bar of unraveled yarn above the dropped stitch and draw it through the stitch to the front. Repeat until all dropped bars of the ladder have been picked up. Transfer the final stitch from the crochet hook to the left knitting needle, making sure the stitch is not twisted (see page 14). When you have picked up the stitch, look at the back of the work; if there is a bar of unraveled yarn still showing, you have missed a bar somewhere along the way. In this case, deliberately unravel the ladder and retrace your steps.

To pick up a dropped stitch on purl fabric, you will need to insert the crochet hook in the stitch from back to front, then draw the bar through.

If in a patterned fabric you notice a wrongly made stitch a few rows back, you can deliberately unravel the ladder, rework that stitch correctly, then remake all the stitches above.

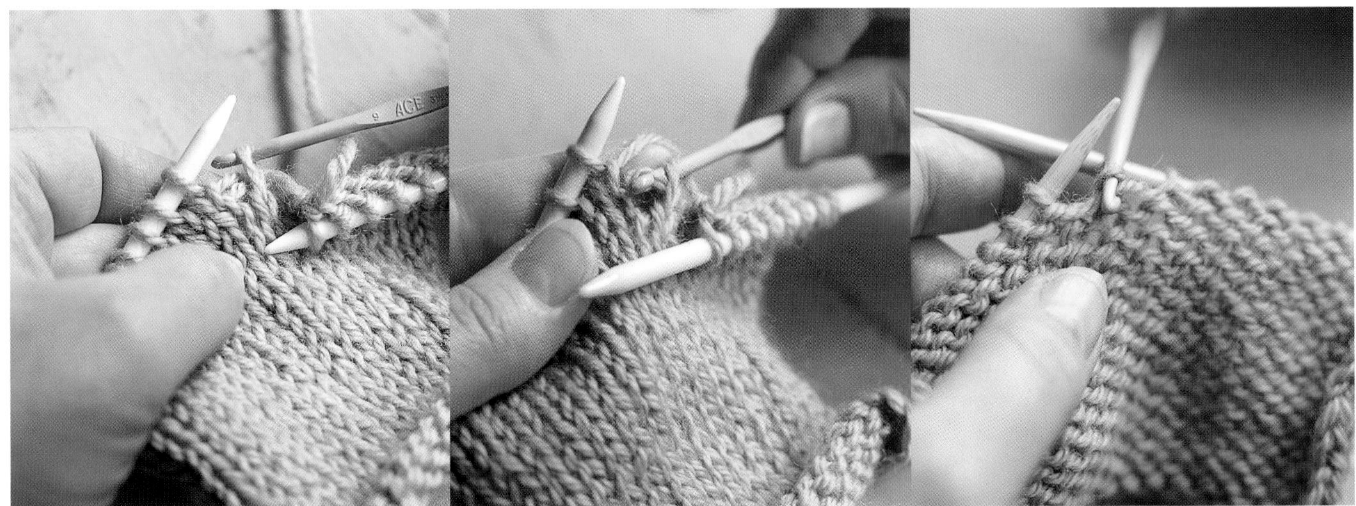

on knit fabric, step one Insert crochet hook through fabric from front to back.

on knit fabric, step two Draw bar of dropped stitch through the stitch on the hook.

on purl fabric The bar will need to be drawn through the stitch from front to back.

Binding off

Binding off is how you finish a piece of knitting. It can be done either knitwise or purlwise, and is usually done on the right side of the fabric. Unless otherwise specified, binding off should be done in pattern; that is, each knit stitch should be bound off knitwise and each purl stitch purlwise.

binding off knitwise, step one Loosely knit two stitches as normal.

binding off knitwise, step two Lift the first stitch on the right needle over the second and off the needle.

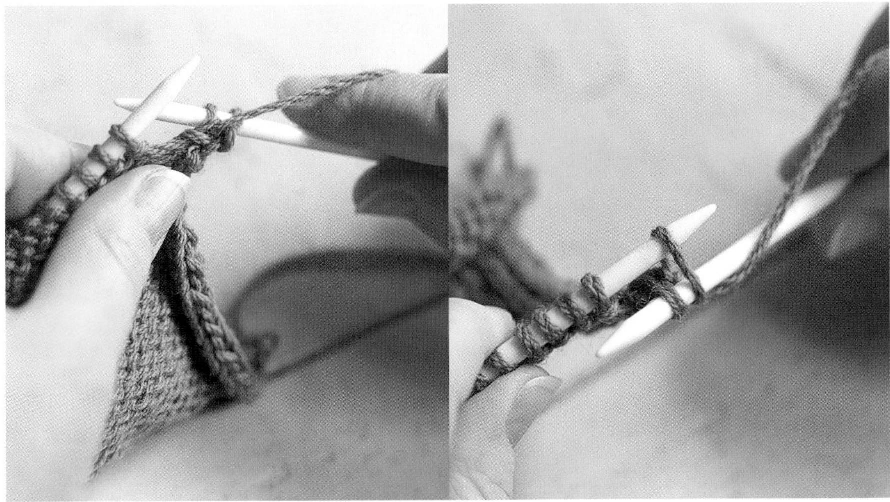

binding off purlwise, step one Loosely purl two stitches as normal.

binding off knitwise, step two Lift the first stitch on the right needle over the second and off the needle.

When binding off, do so loosely; an otherwise beautifully knitted piece can be ruined by a too-tight bind-off, especially at the neck, cuff, or lower edge of a garment. If unsure, bind off a few stitches and then stretch the fabric; the bound-off edge should stretch almost as much as the rest of the fabric.

BINDING OFF KNITWISE

1 Knit two stitches as normal.

2 From the front of the work, insert the tip of the left needle into the first stitch on the right needle and lift this stitch over the second stitch and off the needle. You have now bound off one stitch knitwise.

3 Knit another stitch and then repeat Step 2. Continue in this manner until one stitch remains on the left needle. Remove the needle, bring the end of the yarn through the last stitch and pull firmly to fasten. The bind-off is now complete.

BINDING OFF PURLWISE

1 Purl two stitches as normal.

2 From the back of the work, insert the tip of the left needle into the first stitch on the right needle and lift this stitch over the second stitch and off the needle. You have now bound off one stitch purlwise.

3 Purl another stitch and then repeat Step 2. Continue until one stitch remains, then fasten off.

Pressing and blocking

These methods of shaping finished knitted pieces are not always necessary; check the pattern instructions and do not press or block unless directed to. Acrylic yarns should never be pressed, as they will melt.

pressing Press on the wrong side using a warm iron, a pressing cloth and light pressure.

Pressing

Follow the pressing instructions given in the pattern or, if you have substituted a yarn, on the yarn band. When in doubt, press a test swatch to see the result.

Before pressing, pin out the knitting to the right shape and dimensions on the ironing board. For most natural yarns (wool, cotton, linen, but not mohair), lay a damp cloth over the knitting and steam without allowing the iron to rest on the fabric. Wholly synthetic yarns should never be pressed. Yarns that are a mixture of natural and synthetic fibers can be pressed with a cool iron over a dry cloth.

Pressing is not the same as ironing. To press, put the iron on the fabric, leave it for a few seconds, then lift it up, place it on another part of the fabric, and repeat. Don't move the iron back and forth, as when ironing; this can distort the fabric.

Note that ribbed edges of garments should never be pressed. Nor should mohair, fluffy and synthetic yarns; instead, damp-finish these yarns (see page 23).

blocking Pin the piece to shape, spray with water and leave to dry naturally.

Blocking

Blocking should be done before sewing seams. Follow the instructions given in the pattern; not all knitted items require blocking. However, it is essential for most lace knitting, as it improves stitch definition and makes the fabric smoother.

To block, lay a clean, colorfast towel or sheet on a padded surface such as carpet. Lay the item to be blocked on top of this and pin it out to size, easing and gently stretching where necessary and making sure the sides and ends are completely straight. Spray with water and leave to dry completely. When the pins are removed, the piece should be flat and the stitch pattern clearly defined.

If blocking a large garment, rather than pinning every ⅜ inch or so, it is easier to use a series of straight knitting needles along the edges. Weave the needles through the stitches along the sides and at the ends of the piece, then pin the needles into place. If you block a lot of large pieces, it will be worth your while buying long, thin, stainless steel rods for this purpose.

Finishing

'Finishing' means sewing together the completed pieces. The following two methods are the most common. The yarn used to knit the garment is not always the best choice for seaming; highly textured yarns, or those that break easily, are unsuitable for sewing up. In these cases, use a smooth yarn in a matching shade.

Backstitch

This method makes a strong seam, but one that is visible and not as elastic as mattress stitch (see page 24). This method is best used only with yarns that are DK at the heaviest. For garments knitted in thicker yarns, use a matching shade in a finer yarn for sewing up. Backstitch is worked a consistent whole stitch or half stitch in from the side of the piece for the whole seam. Bring the needle up between the stitches rather than through them, so as not to split the yarn.

Thread a wool needle with appropriate yarn. Hold the pieces right sides together. Fasten the end of the yarn at the bottom of the seam with a couple of small overlapping stitches. Insert the needle through both layers from back to front two rows along from where you started. Take it to the right, across the front of the work, for one row, then take the needle to the back again. *Take it across the back of the work for two rows, then bring it to the front and across to the right for one row, then to the back again.* Repeat from * to * for the entire seam, then fasten off.

Damp finishing

Mohair, fluffy and synthetic yarns, or textured patterns, should not be pressed, as their fibers or texture may be damaged by the heat. Instead, damp finish them: lay the pieces on a damp colorfast towel, roll up and leave for about an hour to let the knitting absorb moisture from the towel. Unwrap, lay the towel on a flat surface and place the damp pieces on top of it. Gently ease the pieces into shape and pin as explained in 'Blocking', page 22. Lay another damp towel on top, pat all over to make contact between the layers and let dry naturally, away from direct sunlight or heat sources.

backstitch Work a consistent distance (one stitch or a half stitch) in from the edge.

sewing up two side edges in mattress stitch (see page 24) Work one stitch in from the edge.

the finished seam Once the stitches are pulled firm, the seam is virtually invisible.

Hints

When sewing together two side edges or two bound-off or cast-on edges, you are working with pieces that have the same number of stitches or rows, so you can match the sewing row for row or stitch for stitch. However, if you are sewing a side edge to a cast-on or bound-off edge, you will be working with different numbers of stitches and rows. Because a knit stitch is wider than it is long, a square of knitted fabric will have more rows up and down than stitches across. This means that when you are attaching a side edge to a cast-on or bound-off edge, there are more rows on the side edge than there are stitches on the other edge. To match the two pieces evenly, make a mattress stitch through each stitch on the cast-on or bound-off edge but skip a row occasionally on the side edge.

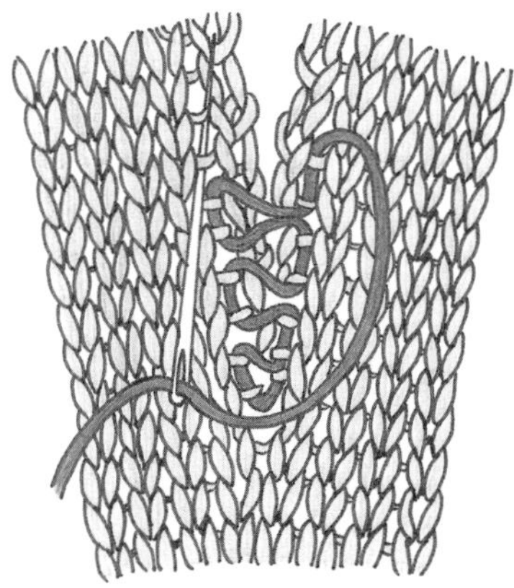

diagram 1 Sewing up two side edges using matress stitch

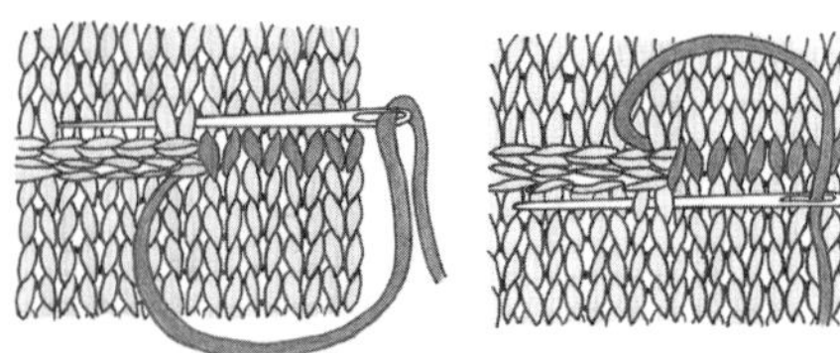

diagram 2 Steps in sewing together two cast-on or bound-off edges using mattress stitch

Mattress stitch

Mattress stitch makes a fine seam that is almost undetectable. It is worked on the right side of the knitting, which means that you can easily match stripes, patterns and textures on the back and front of the garment. If you have never tried it, you will be surprised at how easy it is, and how neat the result.

Mattress stitch can be used for sewing together two side edges (see photograph on page 23), sewing a side edge to a bound-off or cast-on edge, or sewing together two bound-off or cast-on edges (see photographs below). It is shown here on stockinette stitch, but it can be used on most types of knitted fabric.

Lay the pieces to be joined flat, right sides up and edge to edge. Thread a wool needle with appropriate yarn and fasten the end to one piece at the back. Bring the needle out from back to front between the first stitch and the second stitch in the first row. Insert the needle between the first stitch and the second stitch in the first row of the opposite side. Pass the needle under the strands of one or two rows, then bring it back to the front. Take it down into the hole from which the last stitch exited on the first side and pass it under the strands of one or two stitches, so that it emerges in the same place as on the opposite side. Continue in this zigzag manner, always taking the needle under the strands that correspond exactly with those on the other side. Take care not to miss any rows. After every few stitches, pull up the yarn to close the seam. Don't pull it too tight; it should have the same tension as the rest of the garment. Repeat until all the seam is sewn.

sewing together two side edges Used, for example, to sew up two shoulder seams.

sewing side edge to bound-off or cast-on edge Used, for example, to sew sleeve to garment.

Crocheted details

The crochet stitch known as single crochet (sc) is often used to give a decorative edge to a knitted item, or to join together two pieces, such as the back and front of a cushion. Crochet chains can be used as ties. These simple techniques are employed in several projects in this book.

crochet chain Draw the yarn through the loop on the hook. Continue for desired length.

sc around edge, step two Insert hook through edge of knitting and draw through a loop of yarn.

sc around edge, step two continued Draw the yarn through both loops on the hook.

turning a corner To turn a corner, work 3 sc into the same knit stitch, then proceed as normal.

Crochet chain

1 Make a slipknot (see page 13) and put it on the crochet hook.

2 Holding the hook in your right hand and the yarn in your left, catch the yarn with the hook and draw it through the loop of the slipknot, thus making one chain. Repeat for the required number of chain stitches (the slipknot loop counts as the first chain).

Single crochet

1 To work sc around the edge of a knitted piece, first tie the yarn to the edge of the knitting with a knot. Insert the crochet hook into the knitted piece at the same place where you made the knot, one stitch in from the edge, with reverse side facing. Draw through a loop of yarn.

2 Insert the hook into the next stitch or row of the knitting and draw through another loop of yarn (making two loops of yarn on the hook). Catch the yarn with the hook and draw through both loops on the hook. You have now made 1 sc. Repeat Step 2 until you have crocheted around the entire edge.

3 To finish, insert the hook into the first stitch of the round and draw through the yarn. Cut yarn, pull the tail through the loop and fasten off.

Hint

Garter, stockinette, and moss stitches can be worked over any number of stitches, but most other stitch patterns require a multiple of a certain number of stitches—plus, in many cases, a few more to balance the pattern and make it symmetrical.

For explanations of abbreviations used below, see page 29.

Stitch patterns

An almost endless variety of stitch patterns can be made in knitting. Hundreds can be made from a combination of knit and purl stitches alone. Add increases and decreases to make lace patterns, and even more are possible.

Knit and purl patterns

Alternating knit and purl stitches in varying combinations gives you an almost endless range of patterns and textures, including moss stitch and basket-weave stitch (see photographs). It is also possible to 'draw' pictures in knitting, by using knit stitch as the background and purl for the image, or vice versa.

Rib patterns

Rib is is worked in alternate knit and purl stitches and is a very elastic stitch. It exploits the natural tendency of knit stitches to protrude to the front of the work and purl stitches to recede to the back. When columns of knit stitches are worked next to columns of purl stitches, the columns contract, producing a very elastic fabric that can stretch significantly then spring back to its original width. This makes it especially useful for the hems and cuffs of garments, but it can also be used for the body of garments if a figure-hugging look is desired. There are various types of rib patterns. For the cuffs and hems of garments, single rib (alternating

single rib Even rows: K1, P1, rep to end; odd rows: P1, K1, rep to end.

double rib Even rows: K2, P2, rep to end; odd rows: P2, K2, rep to end.

moss stitch Every row: P1 (K1, P1), rep to end (when worked over an odd number of stitches).

one knit stitch and one purl stitch) and double rib (alternating two knit stitches and two purl stitches) are the most common, but wider ribs can be made, and ribs can be also alternated with cables and other patterns.

Cable patterns

In knitting, stitches do not have to be worked in the order in which they lie on the needle. Cables are an example of this. Cables are worked on the right side of the knitting and over an even number of stitches. The cable is formed by slipping a number of stitches off the left needle onto a cable needle, holding the cable needle at the back or front of the work, knitting a number of stitches off the left needle, then knitting the stitches off the cable needle. This forms a twist in the fabric. If the cable needle is held at the back of the work, the cable will twist to the right; if held at the front, the cable will twist to the left. Subsequent rows are worked in stockinette until it is time to 'turn' the cable again. The number of rows between each turn determines the tightness of the cable's twist (see photograph).

Lace patterns

Lace patterns have varying degrees of intricacy, and are made using increases and decreases to form eyelets in the knitted fabric. They are often combined with cables, bobbles and twists for extra interest. Among the many lace patterns are netlike, wavy, scalloped and geometric versions, and those that resemble diamonds, flowers, leaves or intertwining branches.

Right side and wrong side vs. front and back

In knitting patterns, you will see references to the right side and wrong side of the work, and also to the front and back of the work. These terms can cause some confusion to novice knitters.

The right side is the side that will be outermost on the finished item, and the wrong side is its reverse.

The front of the work is the side that is facing you, and may be the right or wrong side of the garment depending on whether you are on a knit or purl row. The back of the work is the side facing away from you. Thus an instruction to 'take the yarn to the back of the work' means to transfer it from the side facing you, between the needles, to the side facing away from you. Similarly, an instruction to 'take the yarn to the front of the work' means to transfer it from the side facing away from you, between the needles, to the side facing toward you.

basket-weave stitch Alternating blocks of knit and purl give a checkerboard effect.

cables Cables can be worked over (from left to right) four, six, eight (or more) rows.

feather and fan This simple but classic lace pattern is made using increases and decreases.

Working from a pattern

Patterns come in both written and chart (or graph) formats. When starting out, you will probably find it easiest to work from a written pattern, but once you come to attempt more complicated patterns, you may prefer to work from charts. One advantage of a chart is that it is a visual representation of the pattern, so it will give you an idea of how the pattern will look in a way that written instructions cannot.

It's a good idea to make a photocopy of the pattern on which you can mark off every row as you finish it. This way, if you have to put the knitting away, you are less likely to lose your place in the pattern. On this copy also write any changes you've made to the pattern, and any notes of things you need to remember. If the pattern gives instructions for several different sizes, you will find it useful to circle or highlight the instructions pertaining to the size you are making.

A pattern should give the finished size of the item; if for a sweater, it should give measurements for the chest, length and sleeve seams. If the pattern has both imperial and metric measurements, use one or the other; never mix them up. Many patterns are written for several sizes. Instructions for the smallest size are given first, then for the remaining sizes in parentheses. If only one instruction or figure is given, it pertains to all the sizes. The pattern should also tell you the equipment and amounts of yarn required and the gauge (see page 30).

Knitting instructions are generally given in abbreviated form to save space. The pattern will explain what each abbreviation means and, where appropriate, how you make that stitch or perform that technique.

When a sequence of stitches is repeated, this is indicated with asterisks or parentheses. For example, '*p3, k3, rep from * to end' means to purl three stitches, then knit three stitches, then repeat that sequence to the end of the row. This instruction could also be written '(p3, k3), rep to end'.

When there are decreases or increases, a figure or figures will often be given in square brackets — for example [56 sts] — to indicate how many stitches you should have at the end of that row or section of knitting.

Read the pattern completely before beginning, to make sure you understand all the abbreviations. Look up any unfamiliar terms or stitches. If attempting a stitch pattern for the first time, work a sample swatch to familiarize yourself with the sequence before beginning the garment itself. It is less frustrating to have to re-do a small swatch than part of a large garment. If you cannot understand part of a pattern, don't assume that the pattern is wrong or that you are stupid; some sections of a pattern may only become clear once you are actually knitting them.

Using graphs or charts

In a chart or graph, each stitch is represented by a single square, and the symbol within that square indicates what you do with that stitch; for example, knit, purl, increase, decrease or cable. Some symbols go across more than one square of the chart; for example, an instruction to make a 6-stitch cable may be represented by two diagonal lines each crossing three squares (which represent the three stitches in each 'leg' of the cable).

Charts are read from the bottom up, starting at the first row, and from right to left on odd-numbered (right-side) rows, and from left to right on even-numbered (wrong-side) rows. Charts show the pattern as it appears from the right side of the work, so you need to work out what stitch to make on wrong-side rows to get the correct effect on the right side. For example, a stitch marked as knit on the chart will need to be knitted on a right-side row but purled on a wrong-side row.

This diagram shows a pattern in chart form, followed by the same pattern in written form. (See p. 29 for explanation of abbreviations.)

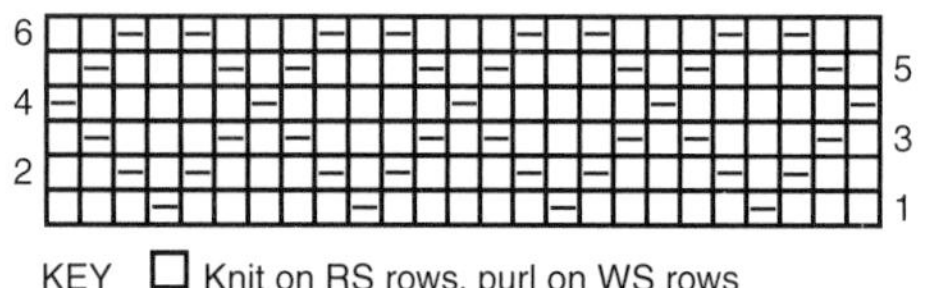

KEY □ Knit on RS rows, purl on WS rows
⊟ Purl on RS rows, knit on WS rows

Row 1 (RS): k3, p1, (k5, p1) to last 3 sts, k3.
Row 2: p2, k1, p1, k1, (p3, k1, p1, k1) to last 2 sts, p2.
Row 3: k1, p1, (k3, p1, k1, p1) to last 5 sts, k3, p1, k1.
Row 4: k1, (p5, k1) to end.
Row 5: As row 3.
Row 6: as row 2.
Rep these 6 rows.

Abbreviations

The following are the most common abbreviations used in this book. Abbreviations that are specific to a particular pattern are explained on the pattern page.

alt alternate
beg begin/beginning
C1, C2, C3 etc contrast color 1, 2, 3 etc (when there are several contrast colors)
C4B make 4-stitch right-twisting cable: slip 2 sts onto cable needle, hold cable needle at back of work, k2 from left needle, k2 from cable needle
C4F make 4-stitch left-twisting cable: slip 2 sts onto cable needle, hold cable needle at front of work, k2 from left needle, k2 from cable needle
C6B make 6-stitch right-twisting cable: slip 3 sts onto cable needle, hold cable needle at back of work, k3 from left needle, k3 from cable needle
C6F make 6-stitch left-twisting cable: slip 3 sts onto cable needle, hold cable needle at front of work, k3 from left needle, k3 from cable needle
CC contrast color (when there is only one contrast color)
CO cast on (see also 'end cast-on')
col(s) color(s)
cont continue
dec decrease/decreasing
double rib 1 row of knit 2, purl 2, alternating with 1 row of purl 2, knit 2, continued to form pattern
dpn(s) double-pointed needle(s)
end cast-on a cast-on performed in the middle of a row: wrap the yarn around your left thumb, then insert the tip of the right needle into the thumb loop and transfer it to the right needle (see photograph on page 82). This casts on one stitch. Rep as needed.
foll follows/following
garter st garter stitch
in inch(es)
inc increase/increasing; or, increase by working into the front and back of the same stitch
k knit
kfb increase by one stitch, by knitting into front and back of same stitch
knitwise inserting needle into next stitch as for a knit stitch (that is, from left to right and front to back)
k1b knit into the next stitch one row below, slipping st above off left needle (to create fisherman's rib pattern)
k2tog knit 2 stitches together to decrease number of stitches by one
k3tog knit 3 stitches together to decrease number of stitches by two
L work loop stitch: see explanation and photographs on pages 70–71
m1 make one (increase) by picking up the loop between two stitches and working into the back of it
MC main color
p purl
patt pattern
pfb increase by one stitch, by purling into front and back of same stitch
prev previous
psso pass slipped stitch over previous stitch
purlwise inserting needle into next stitch as for a purl stitch (that is, from right to left and back to front)
rem remain(s)/remaining
rep repeat(ed)
rev St st reverse stockinette stitch: one row knit, one row purl, as for stockinette stitch, but with the reverse (purl) side of the fabric used as the right side of the work
RS right side(s)
sl 1 slip 1 stitch onto other needle without working it
st(s) stitch(es)
st holder stitch holder
St st stockinette stitch: one row knit, one row purl, continued to form pattern
tbl through back loop
tog together
WS wrong side(s)
yfwd an increase worked between two knit stitches. Bring the yarn forward under the right-hand needle, then knit the next stitch, taking the yarn over the top of the needle to do so
yrn take yarn around needle to create new stitch

Crochet abbreviations

ch chain
dc double crochet (**U.S. sc**) single crochet)
sl st slip stitch

Gauge

Gauge, or tension, refers to the number of stitches and rows per 1 inch of the knitted fabric. Every knitting pattern will tell you what gauge should be used; it is vital to pay attention to this, as the gauge determines what size the finished garment will be. Every knitter knits at a different gauge; some people knit loosely and others tightly. A slight difference in gauge may not be crucial in an item such as a scarf, but it can ruin a garment such as a sweater that needs to fit precisely.

As well as determining the fit of a garment, an even gauge produces a neat, even fabric. If you are a beginner, you may find that your gauge varies from stitch to stitch and row to row at first. This is frustrating, but persevere; as you grow accustomed to the feel of the needles and yarn, and develop a smooth, rhythmic action, the fabric that you produce will become neater and more even.

Even if you think that you knit at a standard gauge, always check your gauge before beginning a garment. The half-hour or so that this takes is a worthwhile investment of time, as it will prevent the disappointment, and the waste of time and money, of a garment that does not fit.

The two gauge swatches pictured opposite were knit by the same person from the same wool, one of them on size 6 needles and the other on size 8 needles. The difference in needle size results in a noticeable variation in the size of the swatches.

Knitting a gauge square

Before you begin to knit a garment, you will need to check your gauge by knitting a gauge square. To do this, cast on using the size of needles specified and the yarn that you intend to use, whether the specified yarn or a substitute. Cast on until you have enough stitches so that they measure about 6 inches when spread, without stretching, along the needle. Work in stockinette, or the stitch specified in the pattern, for at least 6 inches.

Bind off and (if appropriate for the yarn) lightly press the gauge square. Insert a pin a few stitches in (do not measure from the sides, as the side edge is always slightly distorted). Measure precisely 4 inches from the pin and place another pin at that point as a marker. Do the same vertically, placing the first pin a few rows in from the cast-on or cast-off edge. Count how many stitches and rows there are between the pins; this is your gauge.

Hint

Save your gauge square; it may come in handy later for testing how well the yarn washes, and whether it can tolerate being pressed. It is better to risk ruining a gauge square than a finished garment.

Pin the yarn band to the gauge square so that you have a reference of the yarn used and how it knits up.

If the counts are correct, go ahead and start knitting the garment. If you have more stitches than the specified gauge, you are knitting too tightly, and your garment will be too short and too narrow. Make another gauge square with slightly larger needles, and measure again. If you have fewer stitches than specified, you are knitting too loosely, and your garment will be too long and too wide. Make another gauge square with slightly smaller needles, and measure again.

If necessary, repeat this process more than once, until the gauge is correct. This may seem tedious, but it will save disappointment, time and money in the long run.

Substituting yarns

In general, it is best to buy the exact yarn specified in the pattern, as the pattern has been designed for that yarn and other yarns may give different results. However, if you can't find (or don't like) the specified yarn, you will need to find another yarn of similar composition, properties and texture to the specified yarn. Check the thickness; the substitute yarn should be the same thickness as the specified yarn so that it will knit up to the same gauge. You can check the required gauge by looking at the yarn band.

To work out how many balls to buy, it is more accurate to go by the length of yarn in the ball than by the ball's weight. For example, if the pattern specifies 13 balls of a yarn that contains 120 yards per ball, you require 1560 yards of yarn. If your intended substitute yarn measures 95 yards per ball, divide 1560 by 95; the result is 16.4, meaning you will need to buy 17 balls of the substitute yarn.

Whether you are using the specified yarn or a substitute, it is always advisable to buy an extra ball just in case, as quantities of yarn used vary between knitters. Always knit a gauge swatch before starting your garment, so that you can adjust the needle size if necessary.

Note that even when you find a substitute yarn that knits up to the same gauge, the knitted fabric that it produces may not have the same appearance as that of the recommended yarn. This is due to differences in, for example, the way the yarn is spun or finished. If possible, buy just one ball of the substitute yarn to start with and knit a sample swatch to see if you are happy with the look of the yarn.

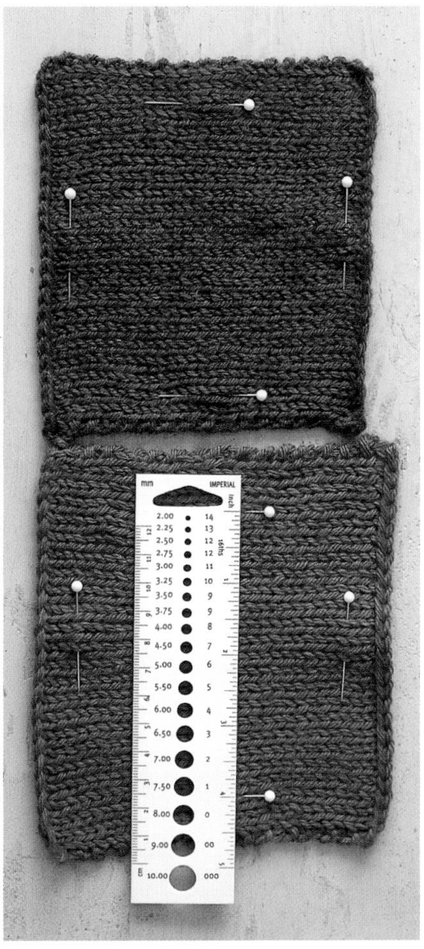

measuring gauge Place pins 4 inches apart and count the stitches and rows between them.

Dyeing your own wool

For some colorful fun, try dyeing your own wool using gelatin crystals. Many people are daunted by dyeing, not wanting to deal with chemicals or possible mess. This method is easy and safe and uses no special equipment or harmful

Materials

1¾ ounces pure wool; it can be machine washable or hand washable (note that this method of dyeing will only work on animal fibers, not plant or synthetic fibers)

1 packet gelatin crystals of desired color

½ cup white vinegar

1 tablespoon kitchen salt

Notes: To dye more than 1¾ ounces of wool at once, double, triple or quadruple all the above quantities. Starting with white wool will give a bright result; for more muted tones, start with cream, beige, or gray wool.

1 Hank the wool; that is, unwind the ball and rewind it into a loose skein about 16 inches long. To do this, wind the wool between the backs of two chairs, or ask another person to stand with their hands held up and apart, with thumbs toward them, and wind the wool between their hands.

2 Tie the hank loosely in 6 places (tying it tightly will prevent the dye from penetrating the tied areas). Tie a contrast thread to the end of the hank so you will know where to start unraveling it later.

3 Place the hank in warm water to soak for at least 15 minutes, or as long as overnight if you can; it needs to be thoroughly wet.

4 Prepare gelatin as instructed on the packet using 9 fl oz/1 cup boiling water. Using a stainless steel spoon, stir to dissolve the crystals thoroughly.

5 Pour the gelatin into a large saucepan, add the vinegar and salt and stir until all the salt is dissolved.

equipment Hanked wool, salt, gelatin crystals and white vinegar are all you need.

step six Simmer the wool in the dye bath for 20 minutes, then allow to cool before rinsing.

step seven Rinse in warm water until the water runs clear.

6 Add the wet hank of wool and enough warm water to cover it. Bring to a gentle boil. Turn down the heat and simmer very gently for 20 minutes. Turn off heat and allow to cool for 45 minutes in the saucepan.

7 Rinse several times in warm water until no trace of gelatin flavour or aroma remains. Squeeze out excess water and roll in a clean, colorfast towel. Remove from the towel and hang to dry.

8 Place the hank onto chair backs or between someones else's hands and wind loosely into a ball. Yarn should never be wound tightly, as this will damage its elasticity. Start by winding it loosely over your fingers for about 20 turns, then take it off your fingers and wind again over itself until the ball is complete.

Colored wool can be over-dyed, for example pink wool dyed with blue gelatin will make a shade of purple. To give a 2-color yarn, tie one end of the hank to the saucepan handle so that only half of the hank is immersed in the dye bath. Or tie the hank tightly in several places to give dye-free spots along the yarn.

simple lace scarf Made using a basic lace stitch and yarn in two gelatin-dyed colors.

Gelatin-dyed simple lace scarf

In this scarf, a new color is joined in at the beginning of every row. Tie the new color to the old using an overhand knot. These loose ends will form the fringe.

Using size 11 circular needles and either color, cast on 175 sts, leaving a 6 inch tail of wool at beg and end of each row. Place a marker every 20 sts when casting on to help count the required number of sts (see page 11).

Row 1 Change color, then knit to end.

Row 2 Change color, then knit to end.

Row 3 Change color, then work in elongated st to end (see below).

These 3 rows form the pattern. Rep these 3 rows until work measures 90 inches, ending with Row 2 of pattern.

Using size 15 needles, bind off all sts. Trim fringe.

ELONGATED STITCH

1 Insert right-hand needle into the stitch as if to knit. Wind yarn around both needles once and then wind yarn around the right-hand needle only as you would to knit.

2 Bring the right needle out and slip the stitch off the left-hand needle.

3 Repeat Steps 1–2 for every stitch.

Materials

Two 1¾ oz balls wool previously dyed with gelatin

Tools

Size 11 circular needle, 24–32 inches long

(or size required to give correct gauge)

SIze 15 needles for binding off

Size

Approx 90 x 4 inches

Gauge

9 sts and 20 rows over 4 inches, using elongated stitch patt and size 11 needles, or size required to give this gauge

Casual bag

This stylish casual bag uses a lovely Japanese silk-mix yarn with gradual color changes that give the effect of soft stripes. Bands of eyelets on one side provide textural variation. Lining the bag is optional, but will add strength and prevent the knitted fabric from stretching too much or becoming misshapen. Choose a lining color that contrasts with the yarn and looks good when showing through the eyelets. If you don't want to line the whole bag, at least line the strap with ribbon to prevent it from stretching.

The back of this bag is plain, but you could easily work it in a pattern or a textured stitch to make the bag reversible. In this case, omit the button and button closure and instead make two lengths of knitted cord (see page 37) at least 6 inches long, attach one to the center of each top edge, and tie to fasten.

Materials

Three 1¾ oz balls Noro Silk Garden, Col 208
If lining the whole bag: 14 inches of a densely woven fabric such as quilters' cotton, 45 inches wide
If lining the strap only: 35 inches petersham or grosgrain ribbon, 1½ inches wide
1 button or toggle, 2–2½ inches long

Tools

Size 6 needles
Size 6 double-pointed needles
(or sizes required to give correct gauge)
Size 6 crochet hook
Wool needle

Size

Bag approx 12 inches square; strap approx 33 inches long

Gauge

17 sts and 26 rows to 4 inches over stockinette using size 6 needles, or size required to give this gauge

yrn (yarn round needle) Take the yarn around the needle to create an extra stitch.

row 14 Purl into the right-hand leg of the stitch made by the yrn in the previous row

Hint

To avoid sudden color changes when joining in a new ball of this yarn, unwind the new ball to a section that is the same color as the last row knitted with the previous ball, and make the join at that point.

CO 55 sts. Work in St st until work measures 12 inches, ending with RS row.

Next row (WS) Knit. This row marks the fold line for the bottom of the bag.

Work second side of bag:

Rows 1–12 Work in St st, beg with a knit row.

Row 13 (RS) Begin to make eyelets: k2, *yrn, k2tog*, rep from * to * until 1 st rem, k1. (See photograph.)

Row 14 Purl. (This row completes the eyelets; see photograph.)

Rows 15–18 Cont in St st.

Rep rows 13–18 four more times. This completes the pattern repeats.

Cont in St st for 35 rows, or until work measures same length as first side of bag, ending with WS row. Bind off loosely on RS.

Fold bag in half along fold line, with RS tog, and sew up using backstitch. Turn bag to RS. Using crochet hook and with RS facing, crochet in sc around top, starting at a side seam and working 1 sc into each bound-off or cast-on stitch.

To make strap, with RS facing, pick up 9 sts with knitting needle, centering them over side seam. Work in St st, beg with a purl row, until strap measures 33 inches or length desired. Bind off. Sew bound-off end

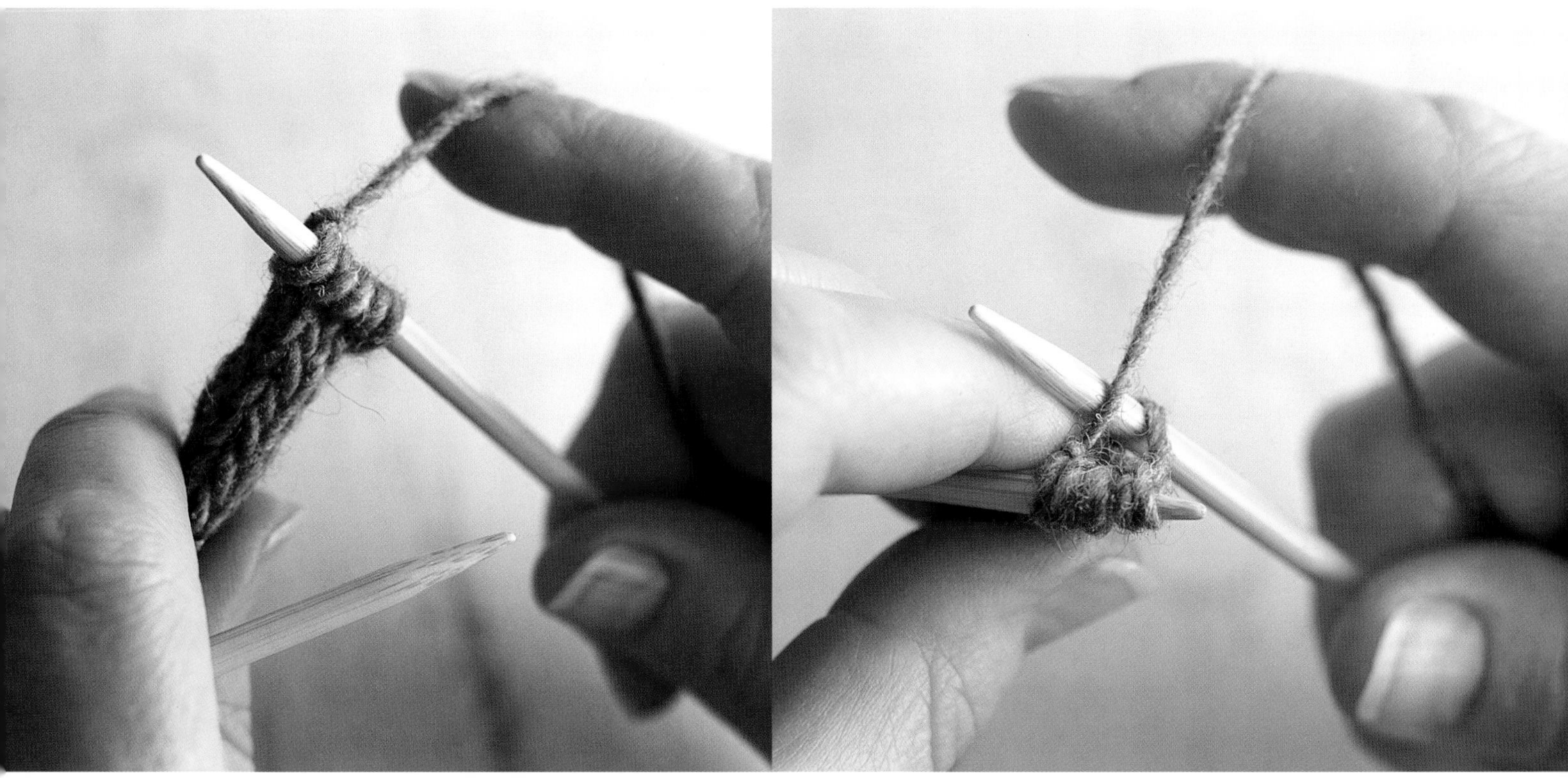

knitted cord At end of row, slide work from left-hand to right-hand end of the needle.

starting a new row The ball end of the yarn wil be at the left of the work.

of strap to other side seam of bag, centering strap over side seam.

LINING AND FINISHING

If lining bag, measure height and width of both bag and strap. Cut a piece of lining fabric ⅜ inch larger all round than size of bag. Cut another piece the same width as strap but ¾ inch longer. Fold bag lining in half widthwise, with RS tog and raw edges even, and sew ⅜ inch seam down each side. Fold sides of strap lining under ⅜ inch on WS and press. With RS tog and matching raw edges, pin ends of strap lining to bag lining, centering strap lining over side seam of bag lining, and sew 1⅜ inch seam for width of strap lining. Fold top edge of bag lining under ⅜ inch on WS and press. Turn lining to RS. Insert lining into bag, WS tog, and slip-stitch folded edges of top of lining about ⅜ inch from top edge of bag, using matching thread. Slip-stitch strap lining to underside of strap.

To finish bag, using dpns, CO 4 sts and make about 5 inches of knitted cord (see right). Sew both ends to center of top edge of back of bag. Fold loop over to front of bag, keeping top edges of bag even, and mark position of button. Sew on button using strong thread. Sew in all loose ends.

Making knitted cord

Using two double-pointed needles, cast on 4 or 5 stitches and knit 1 row. Do not turn the work; instead, slide the stitches along the needle from the left to the right tip. Transfer this needle to your left hand; the ball end of the yarn will be coming from the left of the row of stitches. Knit the next row, pulling the yarn firmly across the back of the stitches as you do so. Repeat until the cord is the desired length. Cut yarn, thread through all the stitches and tie off firmly.

Two-toned ruched scarf

Simple decreases and increases give a ruched effect in this simple and stylish scarf. Big needles and loose gauge give the desired airy effect.

carrying yarn up side of work To do this, loosely twist the color not being used once around the one in use, then continue knitting.

Materials

Main Color (MC): Two 1¾ ounce balls Cleckheaton Mohair 12-ply, Col 260
Contrast Color (CC): One 1¾ ounce ball Jo Sharp Silkroad Aran Tweed, Col 139 Spring

Tools

Size 13 needles
Size 10½ needles
(or sizes required to give correct gauge)
Wool needle

Size

Approx 75 x 6 inches

Gauge

10 sts and 12 rows to 4 inches over stockinette using Cleckheaton Mohair and size 13 needles, or size required to give this gauge

Using size 13 needles, MC and cable cast-on, CO 30 sts.

Row 1 Knit.

Row 2 Purl.

Rows 3–16 Cont in St st.

*Change to size 10½ needles and CC.

Row 17 (RS) (k2tog), rep to end [15 sts].

Rows 18–22 Cont in garter st.

Change to size 13 needles and MC.

Row 23 (RS) (kfb), rep to end [30 sts].

Row 24 Purl.

Rows 25–38 Cont in St st.*

Rep from * to * 11 times, or until scarf is desired length. Bind off loosely.

Sew in loose ends. Do not press or block; damp finish if desired (see page 23).

Hints

When choosing yarns for this scarf, you will get a particularly pleasing effect if you choose one yarn that is mottled or variegated and the other plain.

Be sure to maintain a loose gauge throughout, especially when increasing; tight gauge here will make it more difficult to knit into both the front and back of the same stitch as required.

When changing colors, do not cut the yarn, but carry it loosely up the sides of the work (see photograph above). The natural curl of the edge of the stockinette fabric will serve to conceal the different yarns.

Men's sweater

This simple, chunky, no-frills men's sweater has crew-neck and polo-neck variations. Knitted in pure wool, it will give many years of sturdy service and comfortable wear. The sweater pictured has a polo neck; instructions for a round-neck variation are given on page 43.

The plainness of a garment such as this makes it a great template for experimenting with stitch textures and patterns. You could add columns of cables, make it entirely in moss stitch, or add an intricate aran panel up the center of the front and sleeves. If you're planning any embellishment of the basic pattern, always remember to knit a gauge square and make any necessary adjustments to your gauge.

Materials

15 (15, 16, 17) 1¾ oz balls chunky weight wool

Tools

Size 10 needles
Size 9 needles
(or sizes required to achieve correct gauge)
4 stitch holders
Wool needle

Size

	S	M	L	XL
Length from shoulder to hem	29½ in	30 in	31 in	31½ in
Chest	41 in	43 in	45 in	47 in
Sleeve seam	17½ in	18 in	18½ in	19 in

Gauge

15 sts and 20 rows to 4 inches over stockinette on size 10 needles, or size required to give this gauge

preparing to knit the collar The seams have been joined, with the back left raglan seam left open to allow the neck-edge stitches to be picked up for the collar.

picking up stitches for collar Starting at left back shoulder, pick up specified number of stitches evenly around neck edge, including stitches from holders.

Working with multisize patterns

When a pattern, such as this one, is written for more than one size, the first figure given in any part of the instructions is for the smallest size. Figures for larger sizes are given in parentheses. Instructions that apply to all sizes are given as a single figure. To make it easier to work with the right set of figures, read through the whole pattern before you begin knitting and highlight all the numbers for the relevant size.

BACK

With smaller needles, CO 80 (84, 88, 92) sts. Work 10 rows in double rib. Change to larger needles and work in St st until piece measures 20 (20½, 20¾, 21¼) inches, or length desired, from beg, ending with a purl row.

Shape raglan armholes: bind off 4 sts at beg of next 2 rows [72, 76, 80, 84 sts].
Next row sl 1, k1, psso, k to end.
Next row sl 1, p1, psso, p to end.
Rep prev 2 rows until 30 (32, 32, 34) sts rem. Work 1 row. Slip sts onto st holder.

FRONT

Work as for back until piece is 4¼ inches shorter than back, ending on a purl row. Shape neck as foll: sl 1, k1, psso, k18 (18, 18, 19) sts. Slip rem sts onto st holder. Return to sts on needle and cont to dec 1 st at neck edge in next 2 rows, while at the same time dec, as before, at armhole edge at beg of knit rows. Then dec at neck edge in every 4th row 4 (4, 5, 5) times, at the same time dec at armhole edge at beg of all knit rows [2 sts]. Work 2 rows. K2 tog. Fasten off. Return to sts on holder. Put center 14 (14, 16, 18) sts onto another st holder. Put rem sts onto needle. Cont, to correspond with first side, reversing shaping.

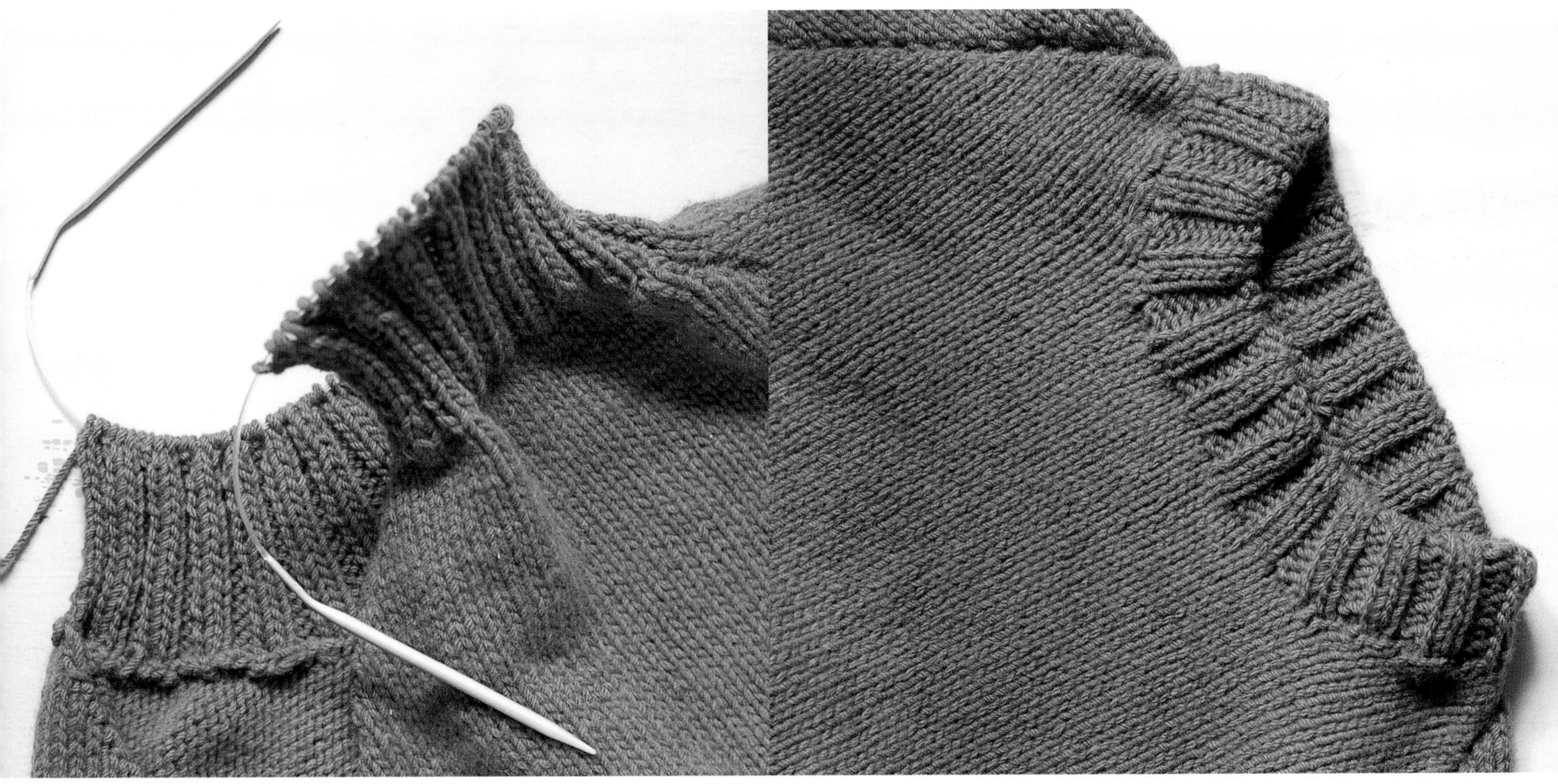

collar in progress Work the required number of rows for the collar variation that you are making, then bind off loosely and finish as instructed.

round-neck variation Either collar can be made on dpns or circular needles if you wish; first sew the entire back left raglan seam before picking up the stitches.

SLEEVES (MAKE TWO ALIKE)

With smaller needles, cast on 40 (44, 44, 48) sts. Work 10 rows in double rib. Change to larger needles and work in St st, inc at each end of every 8th row until there are 56 (60, 60, 64) sts.

Cont until piece measures 17¾ (18, 18½, 19) inches, or length desired, from beg, ending with a purl row.

Shape raglan sleeve: bind off 4 sts at beg of next 2 rows [48, 52, 52, 56 sts].

Next row sl 1, k1, psso, k to end.

Next row sl 1, p1, psso, p to end [46, 50, 50, 54 sts].

Rep prev 2 rows until 8 (8, 6, 6) sts rem. Work 1 row and leave on st holder.

POLO NECK

With a damp cloth, press pieces (except for ribbed sections) lightly on WS. Unless otherwise stated, sew seams with backstitch. Join raglan seams, leaving left back raglan seam open. With RS facing and smaller needles, evenly pick up 80 (84, 88, 88) stitches around neck, 1 st in from edge, including sts from holders. Work 20 rows in double rib and cast off loosely in double rib.

FINISHING

Join left back raglan seam, side and sleeve seams using backstitch. With flat seam, join collar, reversing seam halfway where collar folds to front. Sew in all loose ends.

Round-neck variation

Make as for polo-neck sweater up to and including picking up 80 (84, 88, 88) sts around neck. Using smaller needles, work in double rib for 2¾ inches. Change to larger needles and cont in double rib for 2¾ inches. Cast off loosely in double rib. To finish, join left back raglan seam, side and sleeve seams using backstitch. With flat seam, join collar. Fold collar in half to wrong side and slip-stitch loosely into place. Sew in all loose ends.

Garter-stitch mohair cushion

The back of this easy project is knit in two pieces and the opening fastened with wooden buttons. Crocheting the edges together gives a firmer finish and a decorative border, although they can be overstitched if you prefer.

making up Join the back and front pieces of the cushion by working in double crochet around the edges, through both layers.

Materials

10¾ oz DK bouclé mohair in blue-green
5 wooden buttons, 1¼ inches diameter
20 inch cushion insert

Tools

Size 10 needles (or size required to give correct gauge)
Size 9 crochet hook

Size

20 x 20 inches

Gauge

16 sts and 24 rows to 4 inches over garter st using size 10 needles

FRONT

Using size 10 needles, CO 85 sts.
Work in garter st (knit each row) until work measures 20 inches. Bind off.

BACK PIECE 1

CO 85 sts.
Work in garter st until work measures 10½ inches. Bind off.

BACK PIECE 2

CO 85 sts.
Work in garter st until work measures 25 cm (10 in).
Make buttonholes as follows: (k10, bind off 5) 5 times, k10.
Next row (k10, cast on 5) 5 times, k10.
Cont in garter st until work measures 10½ inches. Bind off.

FINISHING

Place front section on flat surface. With WS facing, place back piece 1 on top of front, then lay down back piece 2, overlapping both back pieces in center of cushion. Using safety pins, pin cushion layers together. Take care to secure the sections where the back pieces overlap. With front facing, crochet in sc around entire edge of cushion through all layers, taking particular care with the overlapping areas. Sew in loose ends and attach buttons.

Snowflake slippers

These cozy slippers for loafing about the house have a snowflake motif worked in fair isle on the instep. If you like the snowflake design but don't want to attempt it in fair isle, it could be worked in knitting-stitch embroidery instead. This simple technique is explained on page 49.

Materials

For child's size: Double knitting (DK) pure new wool, 1¾ ounce balls: 1 ball Main Color (MC), 1 ball Contrast Color (CC)

For women's size: Double knitting (DK) pure new wool, 1¾ ounce balls: 2 balls Main Color (MC), 1 ball Contrast Color (CC)

Tools

Size 6 needles (or size required to give correct gauge)

Wool needle

Size

These are easy-fitting items; actual length from toe to back of heel is 8½ inches for child's size and 10¼ inches for women's size. To make smaller slippers, use smaller needles; to make larger slippers, use larger needles

Gauge

20 sts to 4 inches over St st on size 6 needles, or size required to achieve this gauge

Abbreviations and explanations

K1b = knit into the next st one row below, slipping st above off left needle (this creates fisherman's rib pattern)

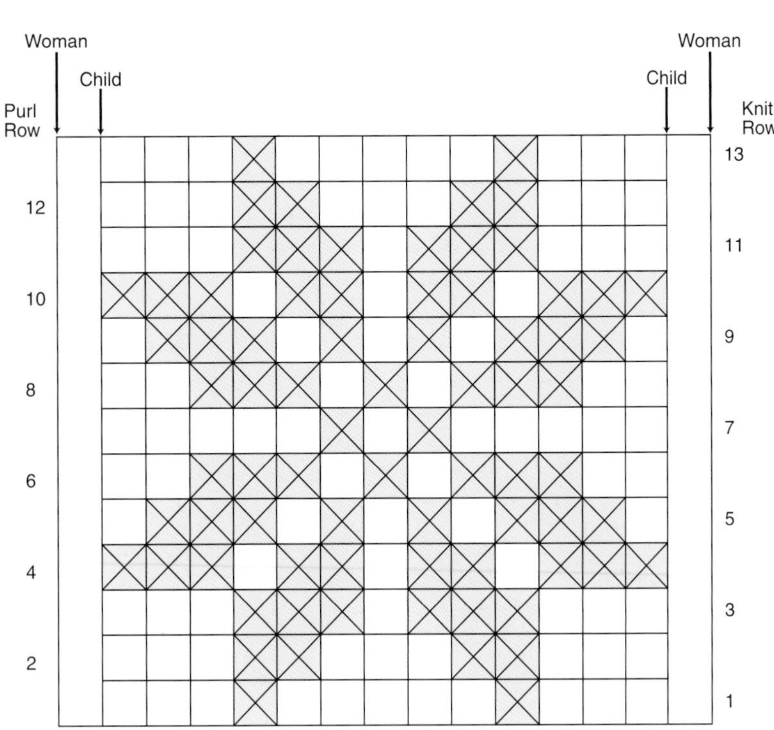

snowflake pattern A shaded square with a cross in it represents a stitch knitted in the contrast color.

knitting stitch embroidery If you don't want to knit the design in, you can embroi it instead (see instructions for knitting stitch embroidery on page 49).

SOLE AND SIDES

With MC, CO 66 (78) sts.

Row 1 Knit.

Row 2 Knit.

Row 3 k1, m1, k30 (36), m1, k4, m1, k30 (36), m1, k1 [70, 82 sts].

Row 4 Knit.

Row 5 k1, m1, k31 (37), m1, k6, m1, k31 (37), m1, k1 [74, 86 sts].

Row 6 Knit.

Row 7 k1, m1, k32 (38), m1, k8, m1, k32 (38), m1, k1 [78, 90 sts].

Rows 8–10 Knit (without further inc).

Row 11 (k1, k1b) until 2 sts rem, k2.

Repeat prev row 5 (9) times.

SHAPING

Note Unless otherwise stated, stitches are slipped knitwise.

Row 1 k46 (54), sl 1, k1, psso, turn.

Row 2 sl 1 purlwise, k13 (15), p2tog, turn.

Row 3 sl 1, k13 (15), sl 1, k1, psso, turn.

Rep Rows 2–3 once, then rep row 2 again.

SNOWFLAKE PATTERN

Note Always carry the contrast shade to the ends of the rows at back of work.

The following 13 snowflake rows are in stockinette, beginning with a knit row.

Follow the chart above for changes of color; sts to be worked in CC are shaded.

Row 1 sl 1, k13 (15) as per Row 1 of chart, then sl 1, k1, psso.
Row 2 sl 1 purlwise, p13 (15) as per Row 2 of chart, then p2tog.
Row 3 sl 1, k13 (15) as per Row 3 of chart, then sl 1, k1, psso.
Cont in this way, with slipped stitches at beg of rows and decreases at end of rows, while following Rows 4–13 of chart.
Row 14 In MC, sl 1 purlwise, p13 (15), p2tog.

COMPLETE SLIPPER TOP

The rem rows are worked in garter st.
Row 1 sl 1, k13 (15), sl 1, k1, psso, turn.
Row 2 sl 1 purlwise, k13 (15), p2tog, turn.
Rep prev 2 rows 9 (12) times, turn.
Next row Knit to end of row [40, 44 sts].
Next row Knit one row.
Next row Change to CC and knit 2 rows.
Bind off loosely.

FINISHING

Using a flat seam, sew heel and sole of foot. Sew in all loose ends.

KNITTING-STITCH EMBROIDERY

Also known as Swiss darning, this simple embroidery stitch imitates the appearance of stockinette fabric.

1 Thread a wool needle with a contrast-colored yarn of the same weight as the main yarn used. To start, weave in the yarn invisibly at the back of the work.

2 Bring the needle out at the base of the first stitch to be covered then take it to the back, under the top of the same stitch, and out again.

3 Insert it at the base of the stitch, at the same point where it first came out. Take it across the back of the work and out at the base of the next stitch to be covered.

Repeat Steps 2–3 until you have embroidered over all stitches to be covered.

This stitch can be worked horizontally or vertically; see the diagrams below.

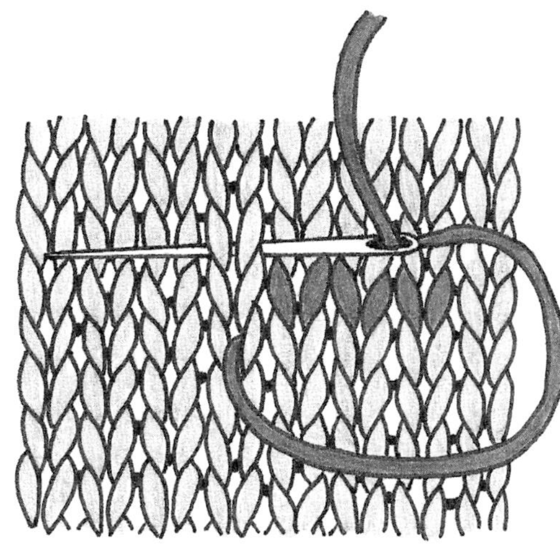

diagram 1 Knitting stitch embroidery worked horizontally

diagram 2 Knitting stitch embroidery worked vertically

Joining in yarn

When you come to the end of a ball of yarn, you will need to join in a new one. Wherever possible, do this at the end of a row, as this will result in a less visible join and the yarn ends can be hidden in the seam.

One method is simply to drop the old yarn, pick up the new one and work a few rows. Then tie a double overhand knot (see Diagram 3), drawing up the yarns so that the stitches around the join have the same gauge as the others. When making up the garment, sew the ends into the seam to conceal them.

For knitting in the round, however, and other situations where joining in the middle of a row is unavoidable, use a reef knot (see Diagram 4) and later sew the ends along the rows as neatly as possible.

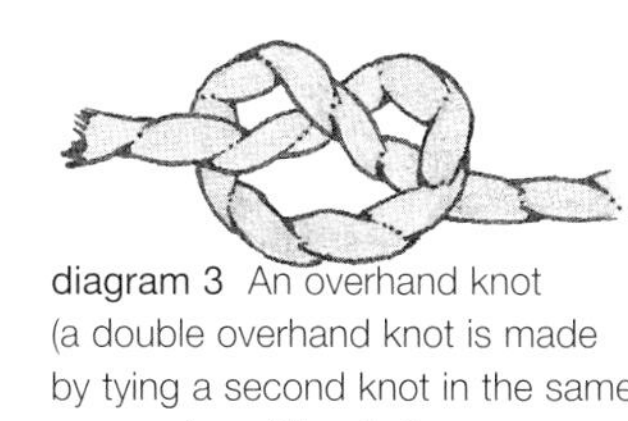

diagram 3 An overhand knot (a double overhand knot is made by tying a second knot in the same way on top of the first)

diagram 4 Joining two lengths of yarn with a reef knot

Hot-water bottle cover

Worked in stockinette in stripes of three colors, this is a comfortingly old-fashioned accessory to keep you cozy on a cold winter's night. The opening at the back is fastened with ties made of crochet chain; lengths of ribbon could be used instead if you wish.

Materials

Double knitting (DK) pure wool, 1¾ oz balls:
1 ball Camel, 1 ball Oatmeal, 2 balls Natural

Tools

Size 6 needles (or size required to achieve correct gauge)

Size 6 crochet hook

Wool needle

Size

To fit standard hot-water bottle: total length of cover is 13½ inches, width of body 8¼ inches, width of neck 4½ inches

Gauge

20 sts to 4 inches in St stitch using size 6 needles, or needle size required to achieve this gauge

back hems Using a wool needle, slip-stitch hems of both back pieces into place.

beginning ties Using crochet hook, draw the doubled length of yarn from the bac through to the front at the edge of one back piece.

FRONT

With Camel, CO 32 sts using cable method.
Row 1 (WS) Purl.
Row 2 (RS) k1, M1, k to last 2 sts, M1, k1.
Cont in St st, inc at each end of every row and making every increase 1 st in from edge as for Row 2, until there are 44 sts.
Cont in St st, without inc further, until back measures 3¾ inches from cast-on edge, ending with a purl row.
Join in Oatmeal and work a further 3¾ inches St st, ending with a purl row.
Join in Natural and work a further 2½ inches St st, ending with a purl row.
Then dec 1 st (by k2tog, 1 st in from edge of work) at each end of next and foll alt rows, then at each end of foll 3 rows [34 sts]. Bind off 5 sts at beg of next 2 rows [24 sts].
Work 3 inches St st for neck, ending with a purl row. Bind off.

LOWER BACK

Using Natural, CO 32 sts using cable method.
Work in St st throughout, beg with a purl row. Then inc 1 st at each end of every row, in same manner as for front, until there are 44 sts. Cont in St st, without increasing further, until piece measures 8 inches from cast-on edge, ending with a purl row.
Bind off.

making ties Using the doubled length of yarn, make 25 crochet chain for tie.

back of cover Make four crochet-chain ties, matching positions as shown.

UPPER BACK

Using Natural, CO 44 sts using cable method. Work in St st until piece measures 4¼ inches from cast-on edge, ending with a purl row. Then dec 1 st at each end of next and foll alt rows, as for front, then at each end of foll 3 rows [34 sts]. Bind off 5 sts at beg of next 2 rows [24 sts]. Work 3 inches for neck, ending with a purl row. Bind off.

FINISHING

Press pieces lightly on wrong side, pressing top edge of lower back and bottom edge of upper back under by 4 rows to form hem. Using a wool needle, slip-stitch hems of both back pieces into place.

Carefully match upper back piece to front, with WS tog. Using mattress stitch (see page 24), invisibly sew side seams, working from neck down to last 8 rows. Then, ensuring hem edge is in place, sew final rows into place.

Carefully match lower back piece to front, with WS tog, sewing up in the same manner but leaving an 8-st wide opening in the center of the base of the cover if you intend to use your hot-water bottle's hook hole. Sew in all loose ends along seams.

To finish, attach crochet ties as explained at right. Sew in all loose ends along seams.

Ties for back of cover

Cut four 71 inch lengths of Natural for ties. Fold one length to double thickness. Insert a crochet hook through front to back of hem layers of upper back, one third of the way across (see photo). Hook the folded end of the yarn through and bring to front, then work 25 chain and fasten off. Rep on other side of upper back to match, and then make two corresponding ties on lower back. Trim ends of all ties.

Triangular garter-stitch shawl

Don't be put off if you can't find the specified yarns; this simple project is great for using up odds and ends. Use a mixture of plain and fancy yarns.

Materials

One 1¾ oz ball of each of:
Yarn A: Heirloom Heatherwood 8 ply (DK), Col 548
Yarn B: Laines du Nord Ombre, Col 512
Yarn C: Cleckheaton Country 8 ply (DK), Col 1962
Yarn D: Patons Ostrich, Col 440
Yarn E: Jo Sharp Silkroad Aran, Col 137 Empire
Yarn F: Jo Sharp Luxury 8 ply (DK) pure wool, Col 316 Jade
Yarn G: Kiss, Col 50
Yarn H: Heirloom Heatherwood 8 ply (DK), Col 583
Yarn I: Heirloom Aristocrat, Col 341

Tools

Size 11 needles
Size 10 crochet hook

Size

58 x 30 inches, excluding fringe

Gauge

12 sts and 15 rows over St st, using size 11 needles and Heatherwood

Using Yarn A and cable cast-on, CO 130 sts.

Row 1 Knit. Change to Yarn B.
Rows 2–5 k2tog, k to end.
Cont in garter st, dec at beg of every row by k2tog, and changing yarn color every 4th row as follows. At each color change, cut the yarn, leaving a tail of about 8 inches; these will form part of the fringe.
Rows 6–9 Yarn C
Rows 10–13 Yarn D
Rows 14–17 Yarn E
Rows 18–21 Yarn F
Rows 22–25 Yarn G
Rows 26–29 Yarn H
Rows 30–33 Yarn I
Rows 34–37 Yarn D
Rows 38–41 Yarn A
Rows 42–45 Yarn E
Rows 46–49 Yarn B
Rows 50–53 Yarn I
Rows 54–57 Yarn G
Rows 58–61 Yarn C
Rows 62–65 Yarn H
Rows 66–69 Yarn A
Rows 70–73 Yarn D
Rows 74–77 Yarn F
Rows 78–91 Yarn B
Rows 92–95 Yarn E
Rows 96–99 Yarn I
Rows 100–103 Yarn G
Rows 104–107 Yarn C
Rows 108–111 Yarn A
Rows 112–115 Yarn H
Rows 116–119 Yarn D
Rows 120–123 Yarn F
Rows 124–127 Yarn E
Rows 128–131 Yarn I
Rows 132–135 Yarn B
Rows 136–139 Yarn C
Rows 140–143 Yarn A
Bind off.

For fringe, at each change of color, knot the two tails together where the yarns have been joined in. Cut more pieces of fringe as needed to fill gaps on this side of shawl, then add a corresponding number for the other side of the fringe. Leave ends uneven or cut them all to same length, as desired.

Notes This is a good item to knit on circular needles, which will accommodate the large number of stitches more easily than straight needles. They will also balance the weight of the garment centrally over your lap instead of hanging lopsidedly at one end, as it would on straight needles.

This garment doesn't have a right or a wrong side; one side will show more distinct stripes than the other, on which the transitions between the yarns give a more variegated effect.

Two-toned jacket

This jacket is knit sideways, from right front to left front, and takes the form of a large rectangle with gaps left for the armholes. The corrugated garter-stitch pattern creates a stretch-rib effect.

The finished garment can be pressed to size, to create a looser fit. A row gauge of 36 rows to 4 inches in the finished garment can be blocked to 26 rows to 4 inches. The stitch gauge determines the length of the garment and the row gauge determines its chest size. The secret of a good fit is to make the back only as wide as you are across the shoulders.

The front edges of the jacket can be folded and pinned in a number of ways to create different collar effects.

Materials

Double knit (DK) pure new wool, 1¾ oz balls:
Main Color (MC) 11 (12, 13, 14) balls;
Contrast Color (CC) 3 (3, 4, 5) balls

Tools

Size 5 needles
Size 6 needles
Size 7 needles
(or sizes required to give correct gauge)
Wool needle

Size

To fit chest: 32 (37, 41, 46) inches. Finished garment: chest 36¼ (40, 44¾, 49) inches; Length 26¾ (28¾, 30¼, 32) inches

Gauge

For the body: 21½ sts to 4 inches over St st on size 7 needles. For the sleeve, 22½ sts to 4 inches on size 6 needles, or sizes required to give these gauges

Caring for knitwear

Handmade knitwear is more likely than commercial garments to shrink or become misshapen if handled incorrectly. Check the yarn band for care instructions. Many yarns can be machine washed, and some can even be tumble dried. If in any doubt at all, wash your gauge swatch to check for color fastness and shrinkage.

Handwashing is best for most handknits. Use lukewarm water and a wool detergent. Never soak or rub a knitted garment; rubbing will cause the fibers to mat, spoiling the look of the fabric. Gently squeeze the garment in the water to loosen dirt, then let the water out. Don't lift the garment up, as the weight of the water will distort it. Rinse once or twice, then squeeze out the last of the rinse water. Roll garment loosely in a color-fast towel, supporting its weight carefully, and squeeze to remove most of the water. Do not wring. Unroll and transfer to a dry towel. Flatten out and gently pull to reshape it to the correct measurements. Leave on the towel to dry naturally, away from direct sunlight and heat sources.

Dry cleaning is recommended for some yarns. Take the yarn band with you and show it to the dry cleaner, and make sure the garment is not hung on a hanger or pressed.

BODY

With size 7 needles and MC, CO 150 (160, 170, 174) sts.
In MC, purl 1 row.
Beg patt Rows 1 & 2: In CC, knit.
Rows 3 & 4 In MC, purl. Work this 4-row repeat throughout the body. Keep CC and MC attached (that is, do not break off yarns); the color changes will be at the hemline of the finished garment.
Work 110 (120, 120, 130) rows in total.

ARMHOLE

Next row (WS) Work first 24 (28, 28, 30) sts of each row for 5 rows, then break off yarns. Join MC to rem 126 (132, 142, 144) sts, bind off next 44 (48, 48, 52) sts of row, resume patt over rem 82 (84, 94, 92) sts, and work 4 more rows.
5th row (RS) End cast-on (see page 29) 44 (48, 48, 52) sts for armhole, then cont over 24 (28, 28, 30) sts, completing full row. Working in patt, work 100 (110, 120, 130) rows from armhole cast-on — this should be the width across your shoulders when stretched slightly. Work second armhole in same manner as first. Complete body with 110 (120, 120, 130) more rows of patt, then bind off in k1, p1 rib — match the gauge of the bind-off to that of the cast-on edge, so that left and right fronts are the same length.

SLEEVES (BOTH ALIKE)

Cuff With size 5 needles and MC, CO 18 (20, 22, 22) sts. With MC, purl 1 row. Work corrugated garter-stitch patt as for body in MC and CC: work 82 (86, 90, 90) rows, then bind off. The stitches for the body of the sleeve are picked up from the long side of the cuff.

Body of sleeve: The sleeve is worked in MC with a k2, p5 stitch patt over the center 44 (44, 58, 58) sts. The sts on either side of this central rib patt are worked in rev St st. Increases are worked by k1, p1 into first and second-last st of 3rd and foll 6th rows; in intervening rows, take all inc sts into rev St st patt.
Work sleeve as follows: With MC and size 6 needles, pick up and knit 52 (56, 62, 62) sts from edge of cuff, then knit 1 row.
Row 1 p4 (6, 2, 2), (k2, p5) 6 (6, 8, 8) times, k2, p4 (6, 2, 2).
Row 2 k4 (6, 2, 2), (p2, k5) 6 (6, 8, 8) times, p2, k4 (6, 2, 2).
Row 3 Inc, p3 (5, 1, 1), (k2, p5) 6 (6, 8, 8) times, k2, p2 (4, 0, 0) times, inc, p1.
Row 4 p5 (7, 3, 3), (k2, p5) 6 (6, 8, 8) times, k2, p5 (7, 3, 3).
Cont in patt, shaping sleeve thus: inc in every foll 6th row by k1, p1 into first and second-last st of row until there are 92 (100, 104, 114) sts and sleeve measures approx 16½ (17¾, 19, 20½) in wide.
Cont without further inc until sleeve seam measures 17¾ (18½, 19¼, 20½) inches including cuff.
Shaping sleeve head At beg of next 4 rows, bind off 4 (5, 5, 6) sts, then dec 1 st at both ends of every foll RS row by p2tog first 2 sts and last 2 sts of row, until 20 sts rem. Dec both ends of every row until 6 sts rem, then bind off.

FINISHING

Sew in loose ends. Press sleeves only. Join sleeve seam and sew sleeves into armholes. The body of the garment can be worn fitted, or pressed to size. The knitted chest size can be pressed to be almost a third larger than its knitted gauge.

To press pure new wool, use a damp cloth and hot iron. Pin garment to size and place the damp cloth over the area to be pressed. The heat of the iron will create steam from the cloth. It is the steam, not the weight of the iron, that presses the knitting. Rewet the cloth with each use. Allow to cool before unpinning garment.

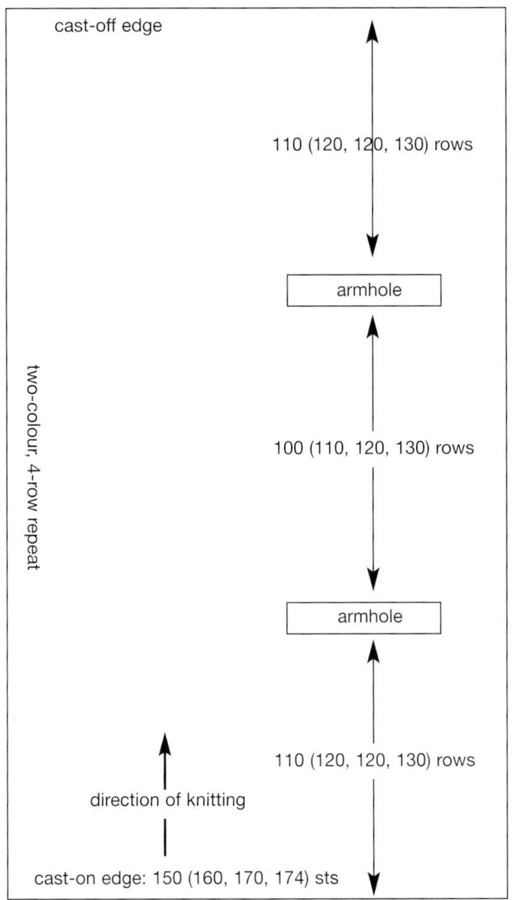

detail of pattern Two rows of Main Color alternate with two rows of Contrast Color.

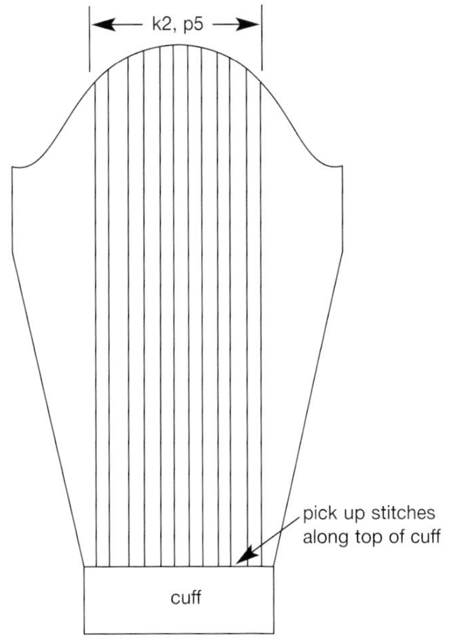

diagram 2 Construction of sleeve

Machine washing

Some yarns are suitable for machine washing. Check the yarn band and follow the instructions carefully, especially as regards water temperature; never have the water hotter than recommended. If you have any doubt at all, wash your gauge swatch in the recommended way; if you are not completely satisfied with the result, handwash the garment. You've spent many hours making it; don't risk ruining it by incorrect washing.

Multicolored beret

This is a good project for using up odds and ends. Use a mix of plain and fancy yarns, and ensure that yarns A, B, E, F and I are DK and will knit up to the specified gauge.

Materials

Small amounts of 12 different yarns. Yarns A, B, E, F and I should be DK; for the others, use a variety of fancy or textured yarns

Tools

Size 5 needles
Size 6 needles
(or sizes required to give correct gauge)
Size 6 crochet hook
Wool needle

Size

To fit 22-inch head. For a larger fit, use size 7 needles

Gauge

20 sts to 4 inches in St st using size 6 needles and DK yarn, or size required to achieve this gauge

Using larger needles and Yarn A, CO 87 sts.
Row 1 Change to smaller needles and Yarn B, (k1, p1) to end.
Row 2 (p1, k1) to end.
Rep rows 1–2 twice, then change to Yarn C and rep rows 1–2 once [8 rows].
Change to larger needles and cont in St st, changing yarns and working as follows:
Row 1 k4, m1, (k3, m1) to last 2 sts, k2 [115 sts].
Row 2 Purl.
Rows 3–4 In Yarn D, work 2 rows.
Row 5 In Yarn E, work 1 row.
Rows 6–8 In Yarn F, work 3 rows.
Rows 9–10 In Yarn G, work 2 rows.
Rows 11–12 In Yarn A, work 2 rows.

SHAPING BERET

Row 13 In Yarn H, k2, m1, (k9, m1) 12 times, k5 [128 sts].
Row 14 In Yarn I, work 1 row.
Row 15 In Yarn J, work 3 rows.
Row 18 In Yarn K, work 4 rows.
Row 22 In Yarn B, work 2 rows.
Row 24 In Yarn L, work 1 row.
Row 25 (Yarn L) k3, k2tog, (k8, k2tog) 12 times, k3 [115 sts].
Row 26 With Yarn A, work 3 rows.
Row 29 In Yarn C, k2, k2tog, (k7, k2tog) 12 times, k3 [102 sts].
Row 30 (Yarn C) work 3 rows.
Row 33 In Yarn D, k2, k3tog, (k12, k3tog) 6 times, k7 [88 sts].
Row 34 (Yarn D) work 1 row.
Row 35 In Yarn E, work 2 rows.
Row 37 (Yarn E) k2, k3tog, (k10, k3tog) 6 times, k5 [74 sts].
Row 38 In Yarn F, work 1 row.
Row 39 In Yarn G, work 2 rows.
Row 41 In Yarn A, k2, k3tog, (k8, k3tog) 6 times, k3 [60 sts].
Row 42 In Yarn I, work 1 row.
Row 43 (Yarn I) k2, k3tog, (k6, k3tog) 6 times, k1 [46 sts].
Row 44 (Yarn I) p1, (p3tog, p4) 6 times, p3 [34 sts].
Row 45 In Yarn J, (k2, k3tog) 6 times, k4 [22 sts].
Row 46 In Yarn K, (p2 tog) to end [11 sts].

FINISHING

Using crochet hook, thread yarn through rem 11 sts, draw yarn up firmly and fasten off. Sew center seam using mattress stitch or fine backstitch. Use crochet hook to weave in loose ends.

Miter throw

The squares for this rug are made in garter stitch by decreasing at the center of each square to give a mitered effect. The throw is constructed diagonally, from the bottom left-hand corner, and each miter is built on previous miters by picking up stitches along their sides. The technique may seem confusing at first but will become clearer when you begin knitting.

When working with several different yarns, as in this pattern, keep track of which is which by taping a sample of each to a piece of paper and writing its name and its key (for example, Yarn A) next to it. Keep it with your work so that you can refer to it when the pattern instructs you to change colors. You could also attach the relevant yarn bands to the piece of paper as a reference should you need to buy more yarn.

Materials

Yarn A: 5½ ounces of any DK wool in Mocha (Mid-brown)
Yarn B: 10½ ounces Sullivans La Vita in Beige/Grey
Yarn C: 3½ ounces Naturally Woodland 12-ply Mohair in Beige
Yarn C: 3½ ounces Naturally Woodland 12-ply Mohair in Grey
Yarn E: 5½ ounces Sullivans Plume in Cream
Yarn F: 7 ounces of any DK wool in Cream
Yarn G: 5½ ounces Trendsetter Dune in Brown
Yarn H: 1¾ ounces of any DK wool in Dark Brown

Tools

Size 9 needles
Wool needle

Size

Approx 51 x 38 inches

Gauge

Using size 9 needles, each 35-st full miter should measure 4¾–5 inches; the various yarn mixtures used will each give a slightly different gauge

Abbreviations and explanations

BY: Break yarn. When breaking off yarn, the tail of yarn can be worked into the next row in the same manner as when joining (see page 64), then cut to leave an end of 1½ inches

dec: At center 3 sts of every miter, dec by sl 1, k2tog, psso (that is, slip 1 st without knitting it, then knit 2 stitches together, then pass the slipped stitch over the k2tog)

Working miters

Miters are made in garter stitch (knit every row) and worked in stripes, knitting 2 rows of each color and keeping all yarns attached (that is, do not break off yarn at color changes unless instructed). Miters are either full miters of 35 sts, or side-edge miters, being half miters of 18 sts. For edge miters (those along the short sides of the throw), CO 35 sts and dec every RS row over the center 3 sts thus: slip the next st without knitting the stitch, k2tog, then psso (pass slipped st over the k2tog); 1 st now remains of the center 3 sts. On every RS row, 1 st fewer is worked before and after the dec, until 1 st rem. This last st is used for the next miter.

For half miters: for the left selvage of the throw, the dec is worked at the end of every RS row by k2tog; for the right selvage, the dec is worked at beg of every RS row by k2tog. Body miters are worked as for the edge miters, except picking up stitches instead of casting on. When picking up stitches, pick up 1 st per ridge of the garter-stitch pattern.

To join colors, knit the first stitch in the new color, bring the tail over the yarn at the back of the work, trap this end in as you knit the 2 next sts, then miss a stitch and trap end into the next 2 sts.

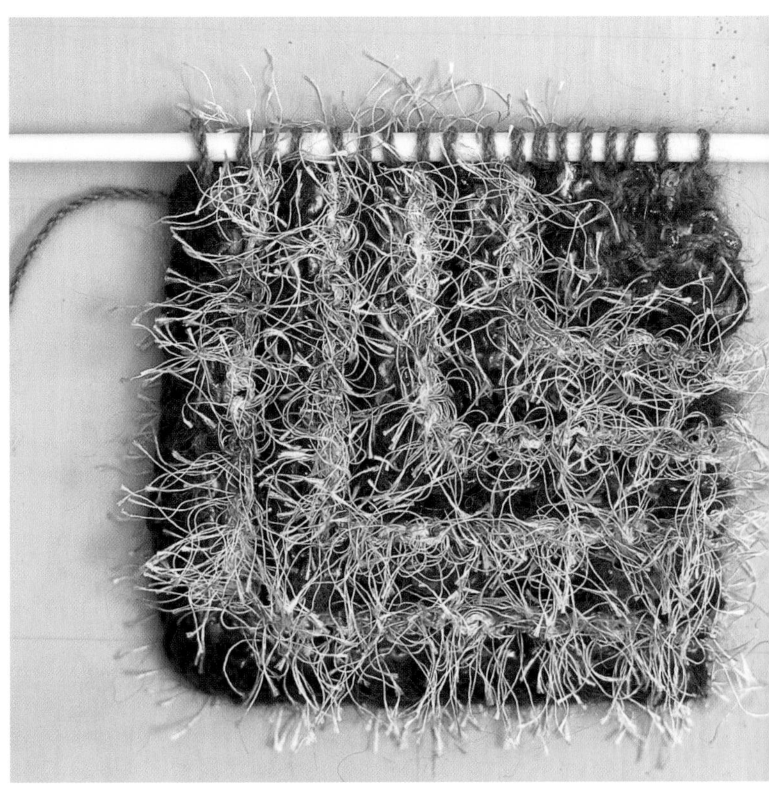

edge miter Constructed by decreasing over center 3 sts of every RS row.

YARNS A,B,C AND D

Miter 1: Edge Miter With A, CO 35 sts; this is Row 1.

Row 2 (WS) In A, k35.

Row 3 (RS) In B, k16; at center 3 sts, dec by sl 1, k2tog, psso; k16 to end.

Row 4 In B, k33.

Row 5 (RS) In C, k15; dec by sl 1, k2tog, psso; k15 to end.

Row 6 In C, k31.

Row 7 (RS) In A, k14, dec as before, k14.

Row 8 In A, k29.

Cont dec in every RS row, in each of these rows working 1 st fewer before and after center dec. Work yarns as follows: 2 rows B; 2 rows C; 2 rows A; 2 rows B; 2 rows C, then BY (break off Yarn C). Cont in yarns A, B and D as follows: 2 rows A; 2 rows B; 2 rows D; 2 rows A; 2 rows B; 2 rows D; 2 rows A, then BY; 1 row B [3 sts].

Next row (WS) In B, sl 1, K2tog, psso [1 st]. Keep B and D attached; both these colors are worked in next miter. When completing each miter, check yarns required for the next before breaking off yarns.

YARNS B,E,D AND F

Miter 2: Half Miter With B, pick up 18 sts from left side of Miter 1 (one st per ridge of garter st plus the extra st from the cast-on edge; 18 sts total). (If making edge or body miter in these colors, pick up 35 sts.)

Row 2 (WS) In B, k18.
Row 3 (RS) In E, k16, k2tog.
Row 4 (WS) In E, k17.
Row 5 (RS) In D, k15, k2tog.
Row 6 (WS) In D, k16.
Row 7 (RS) In B, k14, k2tog.
Row 8 (WS) In B, k15.
Cont dec by k2tog at end of every RS row, as above. Work yarns as follows: 2 rows E, then BY; 2 rows D, then BY; 2 rows B; 2 rows F; complete in stripes of B and F for last 4 rows [3 sts]; BY Yarn F.
Next Row (RS) In B, k1, k2tog.
Next Row (WS) k2.
Next Row (RS) k2tog, pull yarn through sts to bind off.

YARNS G, E AND H

Miter 3: Edge Miter In G, CO 35 sts.
Row 2 (WS) In G, k35.
Row 3 In E, k16; at center 3 sts, dec by sl 1, k2tog, psso; k16.
Row 4 (WS) In E, k33.
Row 5 In H, k15, sl 1, k2tog, psso, k15.
Row 6 (WS) In H, k31.
Cont dec in every RS row, in each of these rows working 1 st fewer before and after center dec. Work yarns as follows: 2 rows G; 2 rows E; 2 rows H; rep until 21 sts rem, then BY Yarn E; 2 rows H; 2 rows G; 2 rows H, then BY Yarn H. Cont in G until 3 sts rem.
Next Row (WS) In G, sl 1, k2tog, psso [1 st]; keep G attached for Miter 4.

YARNS A,G AND F

Miter 4: Body Miter This miter is picked up from the edges of Miters 3 and 1.
Using Yarn A, pick up and knit 17 sts from Miter 3 (including last st of Miter 3). For 18th (center) st, pick up from cast-on edge of Miter 3, then pick up 17 sts from Miter 1 [35 sts].
Row 2 (WS) In A, k35.
Row 3 In G, k16; at center 3 sts, dec by sl 1, k2tog, psso; k16.
Row 4 (WS) In G, k33.
Row 5 In A, k15; at center 3 sts, dec by sl 1, k2tog, psso; k15.
Row 6 (WS) In A, k31.
Cont dec in every RS row, in each of these rows working 1 st fewer before and after center dec. Work in stripes of 2 rows G and 2 rows A until 23 sts rem, then BY Yarn A. Work 2 rows G; 2 rows F; complete in stripes of 2 rows G and 2 rows F; BY Yarn G, keeping Yarn F attached.

YARNS F, B AND D

Miter 5: Body Miter This Miter is picked up from the edges of Miters 4 and 2 and the top of Miter 1.
Using Yarn F, pick up and knit 17 sts from Miter 4 (including last st of Miter 4). For 18th (center) st, pick up from top of Miter 1, then pick up 17 sts from Miter 2 [35 sts].
Row 2 (WS) In F, k35.
Row 3 In B, k16; at center 3 sts, dec by sl 1, k2tog, psso; k16.
Row 4 (WS) In B, k33.
Row 5 In F, k15; at center 3 sts, dec by sl 1, k2tog, psso; k15.
Row 6 (WS) In F, k31.
Cont dec in every RS row, in each of these rows working 1 st fewer before and after center dec. Work yarns as follows: 2 rows B; 2 rows F, then BY Yarn F; work in stripes of 2 rows B and 2 rows D until 15 sts rem; complete in B [1 st], keeping B attached.

Caring for work in progress

Store your knitting in a bag to keep it clean. Special knitting bags are available that have a large compartment for the actual garment and smaller pockets and inserts for tools, accessories and patterns, but any clean bag will do. Or use a wicker basket, first lining the basket with fabric so that your knitting doesn't catch on the rough ends of the wicker. Don't store knitting with the needles stuck through the ball of yarn; this can split the strands.

Enclose the ball that you are working from in a self-seal plastic bag. This will prevent it from rolling about on the floor, getting dirty and becoming prey for children or pets. Leave an opening just wide enough to allow the yarn to be pulled through it. Alternatively, put it in an ordinary bag and loosely tie the neck with string or yarn.

When you stop knitting, even for a short time, always finish at the end of a row; leaving your knitting in the middle of a row will cause the stitches closest to the ends of the needles to distort. If you are going to put the knitting away for some time, transfer the knitting onto stitch holders; leaving it on the needles for a long time can result in a distinct line across the fabric that will be visible once you resume the work.

Using hanks of yarn

Sometimes yarn is sold in a hank – a large, multistranded loop of wool that is twisted on itself. You can't knit directly from a hank, as the yarn will not unravel easily or evenly but will instead become a big, frustrating tangle.

Instead, you will need to divide the hank into one or more separate balls. To do this, untwist the hank and suspend the loops of yarn, without stretching them tight, between two objects. The backs of chairs are good for this; or ask another person to hold an end of the loop in each hand, with fingers pointing up and thumbs toward them to stop the yarn sliding down. Find the end of the yarn and begin the ball by winding the yarn very loosely around your first two fingers 20 or so times. Then take the yarn off your fingers and hold it in one hand while using the other hand to loosely wind more yarn around the ball, turning it as needed to make an even shape. Once the ball is as big as your hand can comfortably hold, cut the yarn and begin another ball.

The secret to winding yarns is always to do so *loosely*; stretching the yarn will spoil it by destroying its elasticity.

YARNS A, B, C AND D

Miter 6: Half Miter This Miter is picked up from the edge of Miter 5. Using Yarn A, pick up and knit 17 sts from Miter 5 (including last st of miter 4). For 18th st, pick up from top of Miter 2.
Row 2 (WS) In A, k18.
Row 3 (RS) In B, k16, k2tog.
Row 4 (WS) In B, k17.
Row 5 (RS) In C, k15, k2tog.
Row 6 (WS) In C, k16.
Cont dec at end of RS rows in same color sequence as used for Miter 1 (except this is a half miter).

WORK REMAINING MITERS

In yarn/color combinations already used, as follows:

.

Miter 7: Yarns A, G and F
Edge Miter In A, CO 35 sts.
Row 2 (WS) In A, k35. Work as for Miter 4, using same color sequence.

Miter 8: Yarns F, B and D
Body Miter In F, pick up 35 sts from Miters 7 and 3. Work as for Miter 5, using same color sequence.

Miter 9: Yarns B, E, D and F
Body Miter In B, pick up 35 sts from Miters 8, 3 and 4. Work as for Miter 2, using same color sequence (except this is a full miter).

YARNS F, C, E AND A

Miter 10: Body Miter This miter is picked up from the edges of Miters 9, 4 and 5. In F, pick up and knit 17 sts from Miter 9, 1 st from top of Miter 4, 17 sts from Miter 5.
Row 2 (WS) In F, k35.
Row 3 (RS) In E, k16; at center 3 sts, dec by sl 1, k2tog, psso; k16.
Row 4 (WS) In E, k33, then BY Yarn E.
Row 5 (RS) In C, k15; at center 3 sts, sl 1, k2tog, psso; k15.
Row 6 (WS) In C, k31. Cont dec in every RS row, in each of these rows working 1 st fewer before and after center dec. Work yarns as follows: 2 rows F; 4 rows C; 2 rows F, then BY Yarn F; 2 rows C; 2 rows B; 2 Rows A, then complete Miter in stripes of C, B and A.

Cont working from the diagram in numerical sequence, in the yarn and color combinations indicated by the symbols.

YARNS B, H, D, A AND C

Miter 19: Body Miter Pick up in B, then knit 1 row in B. Work stripes: 2 rows H; 2 rows D; 2 rows B; 2 rows A; 2 rows H, then BY Yarn H; 2 rows D; 2 rows B; 2 rows A; 2 rows D, then BY Yarn D; 2 rows B; 2 rows A, then BY Yarn A; 2 rows C; 2 rows B; 4 rows C.

The last miters along the top edge of the throw will be worked as body miters, until 1 st remains and yarn is pulled through to bind off.

Miter 64 To make a half miter for the right-hand side edge, in F, pick up 18 sts, then dec by k2tog at beg of all RS rows. Work other half miters for right side edge in same manner as for Miter 64, using specified color combinations.

To finish: sew in all loose ends.

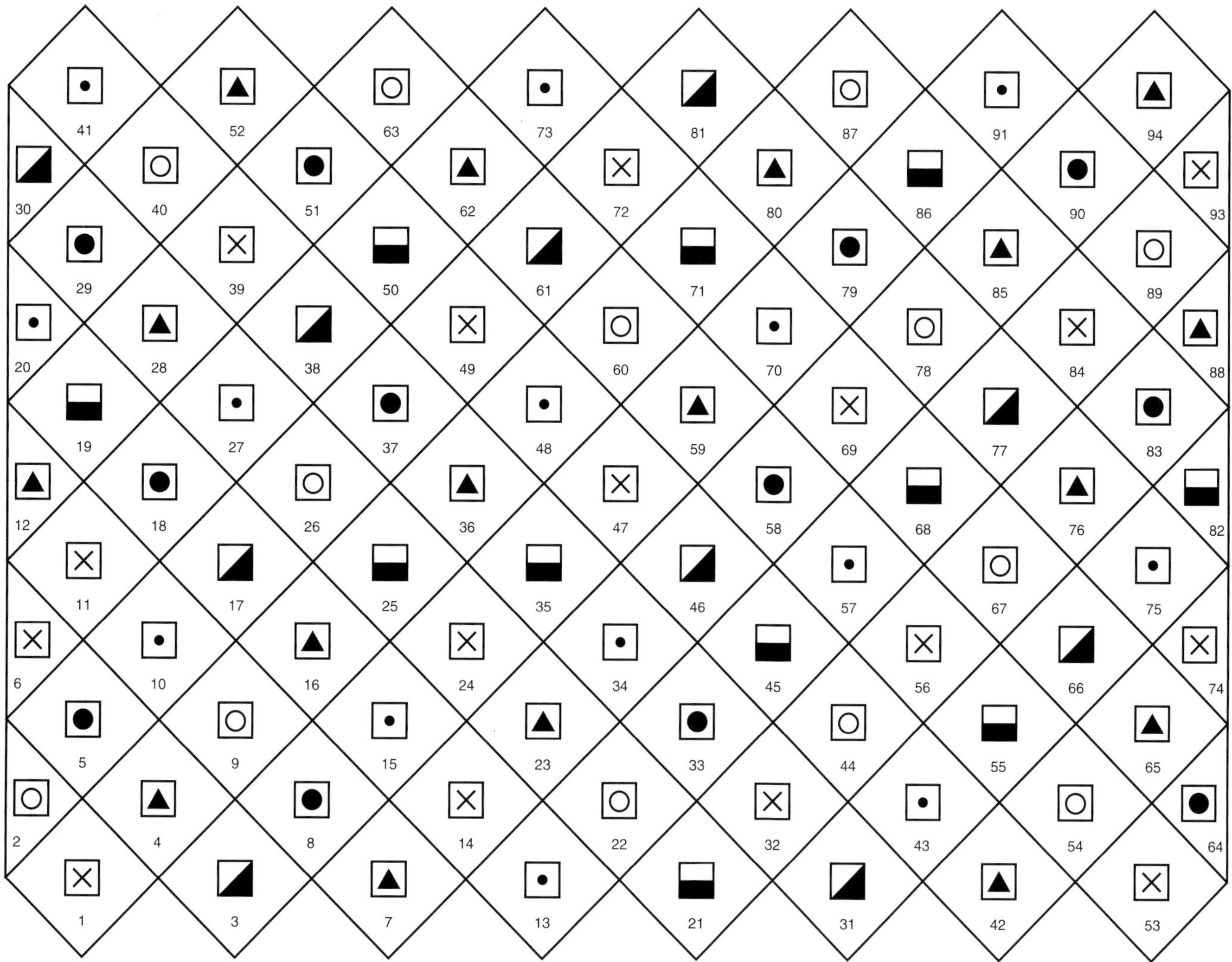

☒ ABCD

◎ BDEF

◩ GEH

▲ AGF

● FBD

⊡ FGEA

⬓ BHDAC

The throw is begun in the bottom left-hand corner and each row is constructed diagonally, with each miter or half-miter being built on the foundations of one or more of the former. Follow the numbers on the diagram for the sequence in which to work the miters. The symbol in each miter indicates the color combination to be used.

Loop-stitch cushion

Stripes of stockinette and knitted loops add texture to this two-toned cushion. Make the loops roughly 1 inch long, but don't worry it they vary a bit in length, as this adds visual interest. Once the cushion is finished, the loops can be cut to form a shag-pile effect (see photo on page 71) or left intact.

The back is made in two pieces and fastened with buttons and simple button loops made of crochet chain. For basic crochet instructions, see page 25.

Materials

Main Color (MC): Three 1¾ ounce balls Jo Sharp Silkroad Aran Tweed, Col 141 Bark

Contrast Color (CC): Two 1¾ ounce balls Jo Sharp Silkroad Aran, Col 121 Parchment

3 buttons, 1 inch diameter

18 x 18 inch cushion insert

Tools

Size 8 needles

Size 7 needles

Size 8 crochet hook

Wool needle

Size

Approx 17 x 17 inches

Gauge

16 sts and 25 rows to 4 inches over St st using Jo Sharp Silkroad Aran Tweed and size 8 needles

Abbreviations and explanations

L — work loop stitch: see step-by-step instructions and photographs overleaf

loop stitch, step 1 Knit a stitch, but do not slip the stitch off the left needle.

loop stitch, step 2 Bring yarn between the needles, around your thumb, and back between the needles again.

FRONT

Using larger needles, MC and cable method, CO 65 sts.

Work in St st for 14 rows, beg with a knit row.

*Change to smaller needles and CC.

Row 15 (RS) k 1, L until 1 st rem, k1.

Row 16 Purl.

Rep these 2 rows twice.

Next row (RS) As for Row 15.

Change to larger needles and MC.

Next row (Row 22) (WS) Purl.

Work 14 more rows St st, ending on a WS row.* Rep from * to * 3 times.

Using larger needles and MC, work 14 rows St st, ending on a WS row.

Bind off loosely.

LOWER BACK

Using larger needles, MC and cable method, CO 65 sts.

Work in St st until piece measures 8½ inches, ending on a WS row. Bind off loosely.

UPPER BACK

Using larger needles, MC and cable method, CO 65 sts. Work in St st until piece measures 8¼ inches, ending on a WS row. Bind off.

Next row (RS) Make button loops: these are worked in crochet chain and sc using MC, with RS facing and working 1 dc into each bound-off stitch, as follows:

loop stitch, step 3 Knit again into the same stitch as before on the left needle, then slip the stitch off the left needle.

option If desired, the loops can be cut to give a shag-pile effect.

(10 sc, 10 ch, 22 sc) twice, sc to end. Fasten off.

FINISHING

With WS tog and matching edges, put front and back pieces together. The lower back and upper back pieces should just meet in the middle of the cushion.

Using MC and crochet hook, with RS facing, and working sc 1 full stitch in from the edge, crochet the front and back pieces together, making sure you don't catch in the loops. At the cast-on and bound-off edges, work 1 sc into each knit st; on the side edges, skip a row every few sts. This will prevent the edge from buckling.

At the corners, work 3 sc into the same stitch. When you have crocheted around the whole cushion, join with a slip stitch into the first sc. Fasten off.

Sew buttons onto the upper back section, aligning them with the button loops.

Using a wool needle, sew in loose ends.

Working loop stitch

Step 1 Knit 1 st without slipping original stitch off left needle.

Step 2 Bring the yarn between the needles, clockwise around your thumb, and back between the needles again.

Step 3 Insert tip of right needle into the same loop as before on the left needle and knit a stitch. Slip original stitch off left needle. You will have created two new stitches on the right needle.

Step 4 Slip the second stitch on the right needle over the first to secure the loop. Repeat Steps 1–3 as required.

Tassel hat

This is a fun, bright design for kids — or for a not-too-serious adult.

peaks When beginning to shape peaks, put the remaining stitches on a stitch holder.

Materials

1¾ ounce balls double knit (DK) pure new wool: 2 balls Main Color (MC); 1 ball Contrast Color (CC)

Tools

Size 6 needles (or size required to give correct gauge)
Size 6 crochet hook
Wool needle

Size

Finished circumference:
Child 4–8 years: 18 inches
Child 8–12 years: 19¼ inches
Adult: 20½ inches

Gauge

20 sts to 4 inches over St st on size 6 needles, or size required to give this gauge

Using St st throughout, make 2 pieces alike.
With MC, CO 44 (47, 50) sts.
Work 24 (24, 26) rows in St st, beg with a knit row.
With CC, work 8 rows.
With MC, work 20 (20, 22) rows.

SHAPE PEAKS

Row 1 k30 (33, 34), k2tog, k to end.
Row 2 p11 (12, 13), p2tog, turn. (Put rest of stitches on stitch holder; see photograph.)
Row 3 k2tog, k to end.
Row 4 p9, p2tog, turn.
Cont to shape peak, dec in this way at inside edge of every row, until 2 sts rem. K2tog. Fasten off.
Rejoin yarn and cast off center 16 (17, 18) sts. Transfer rem sts from st holder to left-hand needle, p2tog, then p to end.
Next row k11 (12, 13), sl 1, k1, psso.
Next row p2tog, p to end.
Dec in this way at inside edge of every row, until 2 sts rem. P2tog. Fasten off.

FINISHING

Press pieces lightly on WS. Using a fine backstitch, join along top and down sides, reversing seams where bottom edge rolls. Using double thickness of MC, crochet two chains each of 42 sts. Attach a chain near each side seam. For tassels, cut six 6 inch lengths of MC and join to ends of ties.

Braided chunky velvet scarf

Made in a thick chenille yarn, this scarf is knitted in three strips, which are then braided together. This design uses a provisional cast-on, a useful technique when you want both ends of an item to be symmetrical — for instance, in a lace-patterned scarf. Once the provisional cast-on is undone, the exposed knit stitches can be picked up and worked as desired. Don't be daunted if you've never tried this technique; it's gratifyingly easy and is explained at right.

Materials

One 3½ ounce ball Rozetti Dolphin in Green

Tools

Size 11 needles
(or size required to give correct gauge)
2 medium stitch holders
Size 10 crochet hook
3 small stitch holders or large safety pins

Size

Approx 60 x 3 inches

Gauge

9 sts and 13 rows to 4 inches over St st using size 11 needles (or size required to give this gauge)

Explanations

To make provisional cast-on, with a crochet hook and smooth waste yarn, loosely work a few more crochet chain sts than are needed for the cast-on edge of the knitted piece. Fasten off loosely; you will need to undo the provisional cast-on later. You will notice that the front of each chain forms smooth loops, while the back of each stitch has a distinct 'hump'. With a knitting needle and the main yarn, pick up a stitch through each of these humps until you have cast on as many stitches as are needed. Work the garment as instructed. When you need to undo the provisional cast-on, simply undo the crochet chain from the loosely fastened end to expose the live stitches. Pick up these stitches and continue as instructed.

provisional cast-on Make crochet chain with waste yarn, then using crochet hook and chenille yarn, pick up 15 sts, one through the back of each chain.

braiding Braid the three knitted strands firmly, making sure they do not twist.

First, cut 6 lengths of yarn, each 10 inches long, for the fringe. Set aside.

Using provisional cast-on (see page 74), CO 15 sts. Transfer sts to knitting needle.

Row 1 Knit.

Row 2 Purl.

Row 3 Knit.

Row 4 Purl.

Next row (RS) k5, slip rem sts onto st holder. Working on these 5 sts, cont in St st until work measures approx 61 inches, or length desired. Transfer sts to small st holder. Cut yarn, leaving a 6 inch tail.

Join yarn to rem 10 sts. K5 sts off st holder (leaving rem 5 sts on st holder) and cont in St st until work measures approx the same length as the previous strip. (Don't worry about making the strips exactly the same length, as you will need to adjust their lengths once they are braided together.) Transfer sts to another small st holder.

Cut yarn, leaving a 6 in tail.

Join yarn to rem 5 sts and work in St st as before until this strip is approx the same length as the previous two strips. Transfer sts to a third small st holder. Cut yarn, leaving a 6 inch tail.

Braiding Lay work out, RS facing, on a flat surface. Smooth out the cast-on end of the scarf and hold it in place with a heavy

picking up stitches Pick up the stitches in the order in which they occur on the braided strips.

finishing After undoing the provisional cast-on, draw a length of yarn through all stitches to make the end of the scarf bunch up, then fasten off.

object. Braid firmly, making sure that the strips do not twist, until you reach the end. Even up the strips by removing the st holders and unraveling row(s) until all the strips are even. Pick up the sts on a size 11 needle in the order in which they fall on the the braided strips (see photograph).

Join in yarn, leaving a 6 inch tail. With RS facing, work 4 rows St st. Do not cast off. Cut yarn, leaving a 6 inch tail. Take all sts off the needle. Cut two 12 inch lengths of yarn, and using a crochet hook, draw one piece of yarn through all the sts. Draw up the yarn and tie off firmly, so the end of the scarf bunches together.

For the other end of the scarf, undo the provisional cast-on and repeat the same procedure, tying off firmly.

Weave in ends of yarn at the start of the second and third braided strips. (Use a crochet hook, as this yarn is too thick to be threaded through a needle.)

For the fringe, using a crochet hook and 3 strands of the fringe yarn, make a fringe at each end of the scarf, pulling through from front to back. Also catch in the tied-off ends of the drawing-up yarn and any other tails of yarn. Knot the end of each fringe strand to prevent the yarn from fraying.

Storing knitted items

Always store knitted garments flat; if put on a hanger, the weight of the garment will distort it, or the hanger may poke through the shoulders. If storing the garment for any length of time, wash or dry clean it first. Store in a cloth bag or a pillow-case, not a plastic bag, as this will not allow the knitted fabric to breathe.

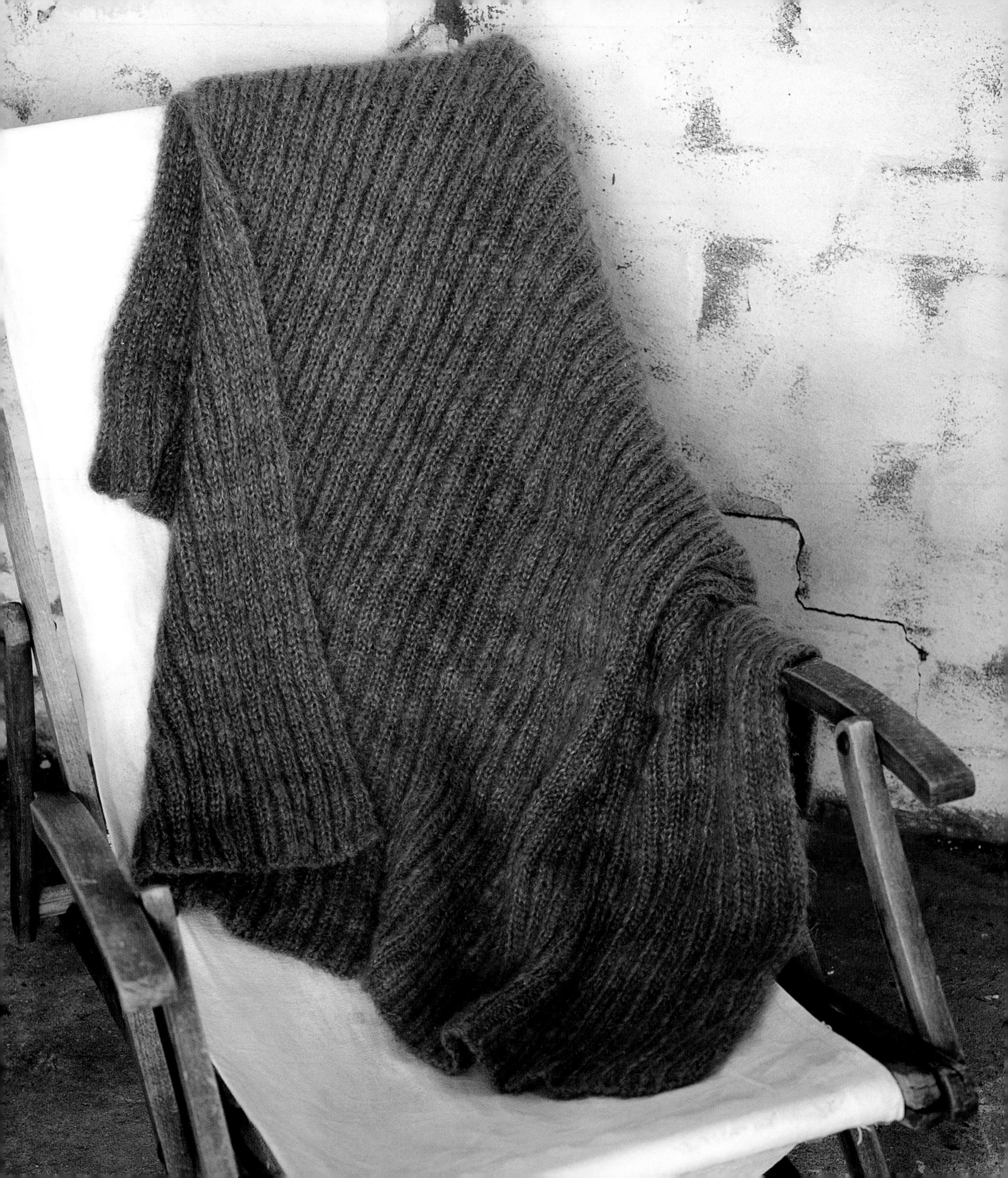

Double-rib mohair rug

This delightfully soft and cozy throw is big enough for a single bed. This is an easy project suitable for a beginner, requiring only a little patience due to its size.

detail The first stitch of every row is slipped to give a neater edge.

Materials
17½ ounces DK mohair in gray-blue

Tools
Size 10 circular needles, 31½ inches long (or size required to give correct gauge)

Size
Approx 59 x 33 inches

Gauge
16 sts and 24 rows to 4 inches over St st using size 10 needles, or size required to give this gauge

CO 180 sts.

Every row is knitted in double rib. The first stitch of every row is slipped to create a neater edge.

Row 1 Slip first st knitwise, k1, p2, (k2, p2), rep to end of row.

Row 2 Slip first st purlwise, p1, k2, (p2, k2), rep to end of row.

These 2 rows form double-rib patt.

Work in patt until rug measures approx 59 inches, leaving enough yarn to cast off and, if desired, to oversew the top and bottom edges. (Oversewing gives a neater look to the cast-on and bound-off edges.)

CARING FOR YOUR RUG
Gently hand wash using an approved wool detergent. Rinse in warm water, then place the throw in a pillowcase and spin it in the washing machine on a gentle cycle. Reshape to size and lay flat in the shade to dry.

Tea cozy

Forget the ridged, ribbed, garishly multicolored tea cozies of the past; this one uses restrained yarns and simple garter stitch for a minimalist take on this retro kitchen accessory. The cozy will accommodate either a round or square teapot, and could easily be scaled up or down. Just add or subtract stitches and/or rows to match the circumference and height of your pot.

Materials

Two 1¾ ounce balls Eki Riva Sport 14-ply, Col 2259

One 1¾ ounce ball Jo Sharp Silkroad Aran Tweed 10-ply, Col 121 Brindle

Tools

Size 10½ needles (or size required to give correct gauge)

Size 10 crochet hook

2 wooden toggles or rectangular buttons

Wool needle

Size

To fit medium-large teapot (6 cups)

Gauge

12 sts and 21 rows to 4 inches over garter st with the 2 yarns used tog on size 10½ needles, or size required to give this gauge

hole for spout Bind off 6 sts to begin making hole for spout.

hole for spout continued Cast on in middle of row to complete hole for spout.

The tea cozy is worked in garter stitch throughout, using both yarns held together.

CO 18 sts.
Work 34 rows in garter st (knit every row), or until the work measures half the circumference of your teapot.

TO MAKE SPOUT HOLE

(The following instructions for the spout hole involve a simple buttonhole technique: several stitches are bound off in the middle of one row, then the same number is cast on in the next row. To cast on, wind the yarn around your left thumb then, using the right needle, transfer the loop off your thumb onto the right needle, thus casting on one stitch; see photograph. Repeat for the required number of cast-on sts.)
Next row k6, bind off 6 sts, k6.
Next row k6, cast on 6 sts by method described above, k6.
Cont in garter st for another 34 rows, or until work measures same length as previous side. Bind off.

Join 2 ends tog on WS, leaving enough room for the teapot handle. Measure the distance between the top of the work and the top of the handle, and stitch accordingly. Do the same with the bottom. Weave in any loose ends with a wool needle.

making up Sew up the ends, leaving a hole large enough for the pot's handle.

finishing lid Fasten the toggles on the lid through the crochet chain loops.

BUTTON LOOPS

Using both yarns held together and crochet hook, insert hook into fabric of tea cozy on RS, about 2 inches down from top and in center of one side. Take hook under one knitted row then up to RS and pull yarns through, leaving a tail on WS of about 6 inches. Make 12 chain. End with slip stitch into first chain to make button loop thus: insert needle into first chain that you made, then pull yarn through. Cut yarn, leaving 6 inches, and pull tail of yarn through loop on hook to fasten off. Draw all tails of yarn to WS and tie off firmly. With wool needle, weave in loose ends.
Repeat for second loop on other side.

TO MAKE LID

Using both yarns held together, as before, CO 16 sts.
Work 25 rows in garter st.
Bind off.

Sew toggles or buttons onto opposite corners of lid. Attach the lid to the teapot so that it sits diagonally across the top.

Hiding tails of yarn

Once your knitting is finished, there will be tails of yarn, from cast-on or bound-off edges or yarn changes, that need to be concealed. Where these occur at the beginning or end of a row, sew them into the finished seams on the wrong side, using a wool needle. If the tails occur in the middle of a row, weave them into the knitting on the wrong side, using a wool needle and taking care that the woven-in strands do not show through to the right side.

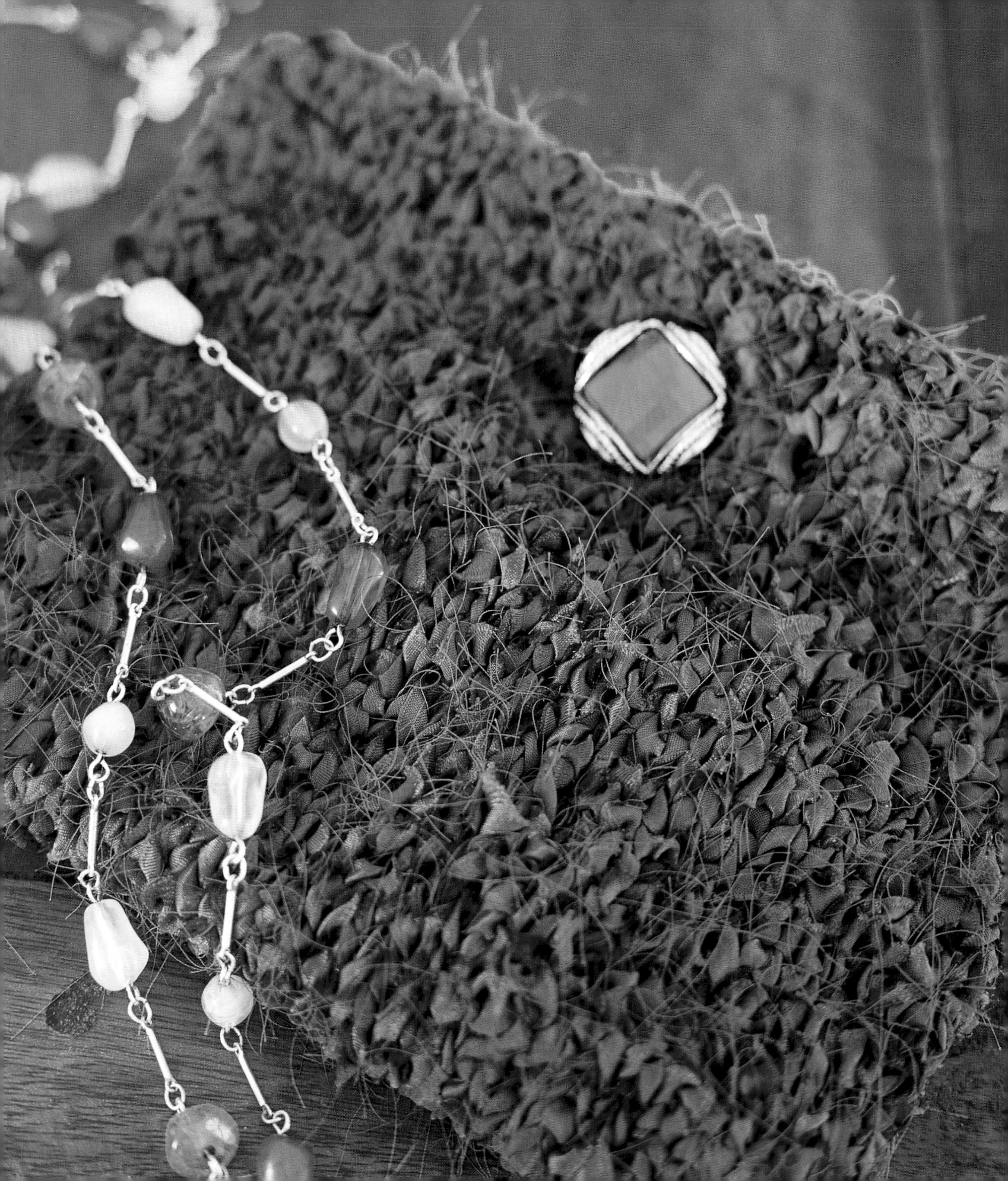

Clutch purse

This simple evening bag in stockinette is made from strips of satin fabric.

cutting fabric Cut strips of fabric about 1⁄4 inch wide, ending each cut just before the edge to create one continuous strip.

Materials

40 inches polyester satin, 44 inches wide
Matching sewing thread
1 inch button

Tools

Size 10 needles

Size

Approx 5½ x 7½ inches

Gauge

16 sts and 19 rows to 4 inches over St st using size 10 needles

Cut 32 inches of the fabric into a continuous strip (see right). CO 29 sts.

Row 1 (RS) Knit.

Row 2 Purl.

Cont in St st until work measures approx 14½ inches, ending with a WS row.

Next row Make buttonhole: k14, bind off 3 sts, k to end.

Next row p 13, cast on 3 sts, p to end.

Work 8 more rows St st. Bind off on RS.

FINISHING

Fold back 4 rows at each end to form facing. Slip-stitch into place on WS using matching sewing thread, taking care to leave buttonhole open. Fold bag in half, WS tog. Using a doubled length of sewing thread, oversew side seams tog on RS using very small stitches; they should be hardly visible against the texture of the knitting.

LINING

From remaining fabric, cut a piece the width of the finished bag by twice its length, plus 3⁄8 inch all round. Fold in half, RS tog, and sew 3⁄8 inch seam down each side. Fold down 3⁄8 inch all around top edge and press. In lining, make buttonhole slightly larger than that of buttonhole in bag, matching their positions. Put lining inside bag, with WS tog, and slip-stitch into place at top edge. Slip-stitch edges of both buttonholes together. Mark position of button and sew into place on inside of bag.

Cutting strips

Across width of fabric, make cuts approx 1⁄4 inch wide (do not worry if they vary a little). Do not cut to the very edge; end each cut about 3⁄4 inch from edge (see photograph), and start another cut 1⁄4 inch from that point. Cut off corners at end of each strip, as shown. Repeat until you have cut about 32 inches of the fabric. (Begin winding the strip into a ball once you have made several cuts; continue winding after every few cuts.)

Pure silk top and tie-front jacket

The semifitted sleeveless top, worked in stockinette, has gentle side shaping and a ladder-stitch panel at the front yoke. The jacket features extended fronts that may be tied at center front, left open, or wrapped and fastened. The bottom of the sleeve is gently flared, with a notched detail at the seam. The jacket back is worked in stockinette, with the fronts and sleeves in ladder stitch. A picot trim in crochet finishes all edges of both garments.

The ladder-stitch pattern has been devised so that when the designated stitch is dropped, it will ladder down only until it is stopped by a yarn forward of a prior row. The fabric then becomes quite organic as the stitches around the ladder start to move and enlarge as they take up the excess yarn from the ladder.

Materials

100% pure silk tape, 1¾ ounce balls, in color Natural: for top, 3 (3, 3) balls; for jacket, 5 (6, 7) balls (such as Tussah Tape, available from www.sarahdurrant.com)

Tools

Size 9 knitting needles (or size required to give correct gauge)
Size 8 crochet hook
Stitch holders
Wool needle

Size

To fit bust size		
34–36 in	38–40 in	42–44 in
Top measures at bustline		
37½ in	41½ in	46 in
Length of top from shoulder		
19½ in	21 in	22 in
Jacket measures at bustline		
40 in	44 in	47½ in
Length of jacket from shoulder		
21¾ in	23 in	24 in
Jacket sleeve seam		
17 in	17 in	17 in

Gauge

17 sts and 21 rows to 4 inches over St st, and 16 sts and 20 rows to 4 inches over ladder st using size 9 needles, or size required to give this gauge

Hints

All shaping in these garments is worked decoratively, several stitches in from the end of the row. The top is recommended as an intermediate knit, with the jacket being more suited to advanced knitters.

While the pattern positioning is set for each piece, the knitter will have to make judgments concerning patterning within shaped sections; likewise, the shaping for the fronts requires a number of functions to be carried out at the same time.

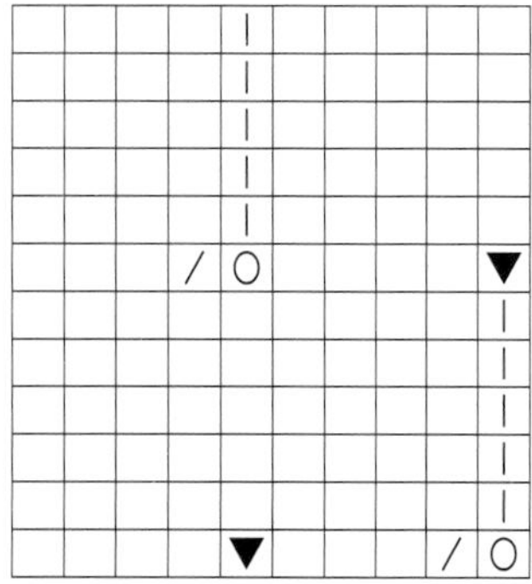

1 patt rep = 10 sts x 12 rows
Odd-numbered rows are RS rows, read right to left
Even-numbered rows are WS rows, read left to right

Pattern notes

Read complete pattern instructions prior to commencing work.

The pattern is positioned by the pattern set-up row in the written instructions. The pattern repeat is as shown in the chart below. To make ladder, slide stitch marked off needle and allow to ladder until halted by the yfwd of 6 rows below (always check that you are dropping the correct stitch), then replace top ladder bar onto left needle and knit off as normal. When working in ladder stitch pattern, maintain pattern placement as set, but always keep at least 3 sts in St st at edges of work when shaping. Thus it is sometimes necessary to drop a pattern st a row or two before the usual 1st or 7th row, but drop *only* the stitch(es) affected, and complete the remainder of the row as charted.

It is recommended that you use a backward loop or a provisional cast-on (see page 74) for this project.

All decs on both garments are worked on the 4th st in from the edge.

For dec on left-hand edge of work: For RS rows, work to last 5 sts, k2tog tbl, k3. For WS rows: p3, p2tog tbl, work in patt to end.

For dec on right-hand edge of work: For RS rows, K3, k2tog, work in patt to end. For WS rows: work to last 5 sts, p2tog, p3.

☐ k on RS, p on WS rows

| worked as above, then unravelled at row 1 or 7

/ k2tog

O yarn forward

▼ make ladder (see pattern notes, above)

Sleeveless top

FRONT

*Using size 9 needles, CO 81 (89, 99) sts.

Beg with a knit row (RS), cont in St st until work measures 3½ (4, 4¼) inches from beg, ending after a WS row.

Shape waist as follows:

Next row k3, k2tog, k to last 5 sts, k2tog tbl, k3.

Working decs as set by last row, dec 1 st at each end of every foll 6th row until 75 (83, 93) sts rem.

Work 11 rows straight, ending after a WS row.

Next row k3, m1, k to last 3 sts, m1, k3.

Working incs as set by last row, inc 1 st at each end of every foll 6th row until 81 (89, 99) sts rem. Cont straight until work measures 10½ (11, 11½) inches, ending after a WS row.

Next row (This row sets up the pattern, and is worked once only, in lieu of row 1 of chart): k5 (4, 4) *yfwd, k2tog, k8; rep from * to last 6 (5, 5) sts, yfwd, k2tog, k4 (3, 3).

Note: the first yfwd corresponds to the first st of row 1 of chart and the edge sts are not shown on chart. Beg with row 2 of chart and cont in ladder st patt as set until work measures 12 (13, 13¾) inches, ending after a WS row.

SHAPE ARMHOLES

Cast off 3 (4, 4) sts at beg of next 2 rows, then 2 (3, 3) sts at beg of foll 2 rows. Dec 1 st at both ends of foll 4 rows, then 1 st at both ends of foll 2 (2, 4) alt rows. Dec 1 st at both ends of next 4th row [57, 61, 67 sts].**

Cont in patt until armhole measures 4 (4¼, 4¾) inches, ending after a WS row.

SHAPE NECK

Next row Work first 23 (25, 28) sts, turn and place rem sts on a holder.

Complete left front neckline as follows: Bind off 3 sts at neck edge on next row and foll alt row. Bind off 2 sts at beg of next alt row, and dec 1 st at neck edge at beginning of foll 3 alt rows. Work straight until armhole measures 7½ (8, 8¼) inches. Bind off remaining 12 (14, 17) sts loosely.

Rejoin yarn to 23 (25, 28) sts on right side of neckline, leaving the 11 sts of center neck on the holder, and complete to match left side, reversing shapings as necessary.

BACK

Work as front from * to ** but in St st throughout (that is, no patterned yoke). Cont straight until armhole measures 6 (6¼, 6¾) inches, ending after a WS row.

SHAPE BACK NECK

Next row Work first 20 (22, 25) sts. Turn and place rem sts on a holder. Cast off 3 sts at neck edge at beg of next row and 2 sts at beg of foll alt row. Dec 1 st at neck edge on next 3 rows. Work 1 row, then bind off rem 12 (14, 17) sts loosely. Leaving 17 sts on holder for center neckline, rejoin yarn and complete second side to match, reversing shapings where necessary.

FINISHING

Carefully block all pieces to size, using a warm steam iron on WS, held above work to avoid flattening fabric. Neatly join shoulder seams. Working from the RS, join side seams using mattress stitch, working 1 st in from side edge and taking care to match decs.

TRIM

From RS, using size 8 crochet hook, work 1 round of sc around lower edge, working 1 sc into every st of cast-on row, and joining round with a slip stitch.

Next round (picot edge): 2 ch, *work 1 sl st into each of the next 2 sc, 3 ch, work 1 sl st into next sc**. Rep from * to ** to end of round, joining with a sl st to finish.

Apply these 2 rounds of trim to armhole and neckline, taking live sts off holder as you work and, where necessary, dec sts at inner curves to ensure trim remains firm and flat. Give the trim a final light press.

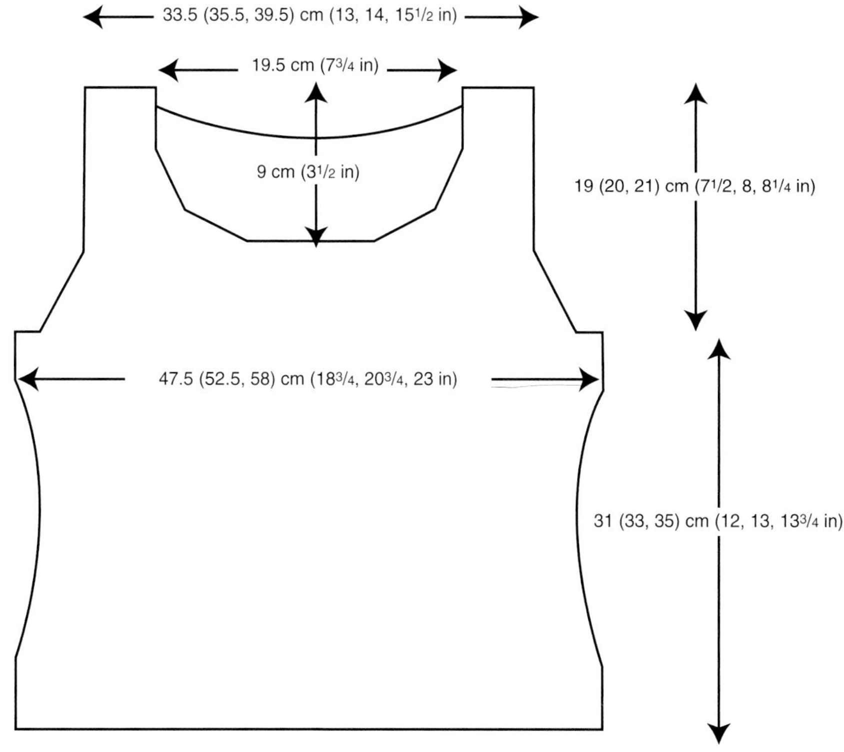

Schematic – Top

Tie-front jacket

JACKET BACK

Using size 9 needles, CO 87 (95, 103) sts. It is recommended that you use a backward loop or a provisional cast-on (see page 74) for this project.

Beg with a knit row (RS) and working in St st throughout, cont until work measures 13¾ (14½, 15½) inches, ending after a WS row.

SHAPE ARMHOLES

Bind off 4 (4, 5) sts at beg of next 2 rows, then dec 1 st at each end of next 1 (4, 4) rows. Then dec 1 st at each end of foll alt rows 6 (5, 7) times in all [65, 69, 71 sts].

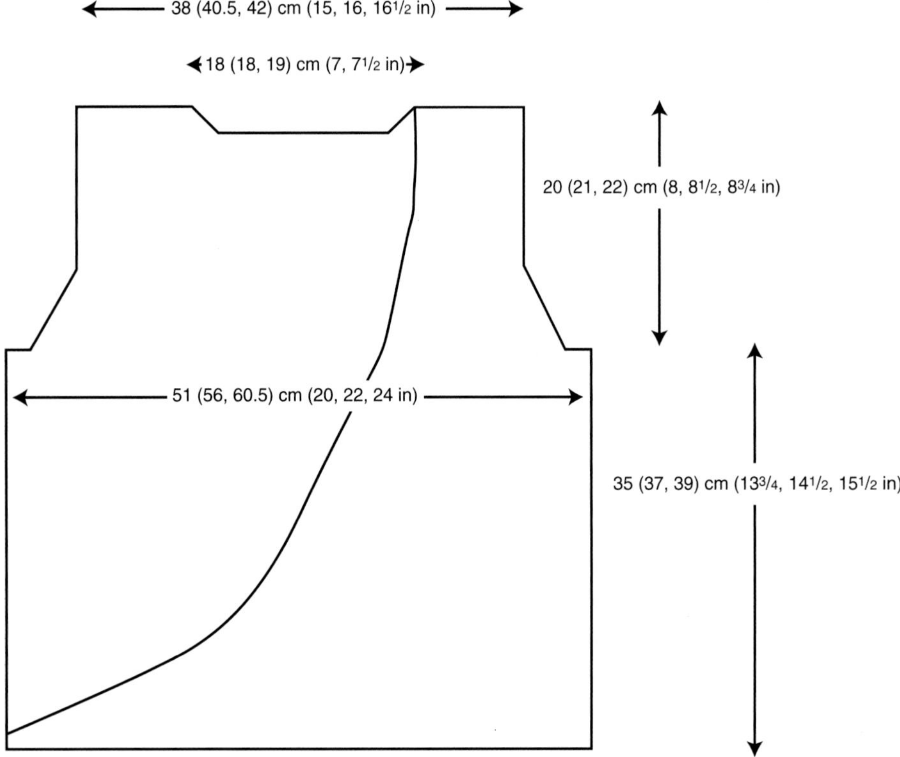

Schematic – Jacket back and one front

Cont straight until armhole measures 7 (7½, 8) inches, ending after a WS row.

SHAPE BACK NECK

Next row Work first 20 (22, 22) sts. Turn and place rem sts on a holder. Dec 1 st at neck edge on next 3 rows. Work 1 row then bind off rem 17 (19, 19) sts loosely. Leaving 25 (25, 27) sts on holder for center neckline, rejoin yarn and complete second side to match, reversing shapings where necessary.

JACKET LEFT FRONT

(Worked in ladder st patt.)

CO 85 (93, 101) sts and, beg with a knit row (RS), work 2 rows St st.

Next row (this is pattern set-up row): k3, *yfwd, k2tog, k8. Rep from * to last 2 (0, 8) sts then, for 1st size only, k2. For 3rd size only, yfwd, k2tog, k6.

Note: the first yfwd corresponds to the first st of row 1 of chart and the edge sts are not shown on chart.

Beg with row 2 of chart, cont in ladder st patt as set, and commence neckline slope shaping on next row, as follows: dec 1 st at neck edge on every row 24 (28, 32) times, then every foll 2nd and 3rd row 11 times [39, 43, 47 sts]. Then dec 1 st at neck edge on each alt row 7 times, and 1 st on every foll 4th row 4 (4, 5) times. *At the same time*, when work measures 13¾ (14½, 15½) in, work armhole shaping as for back [17, 19, 19 sts].

Cont in patt until armhole measures same as for back to shoulder, then bind off all sts loosely.

RIGHT FRONT

Complete to match left front, reversing shapings, and noting that pattern set-up row will be as follows: k11 (9, 7) sts, *yfwd, k2tog, k8. Rep from * to last 4 sts, yfwd, k2tog, k2.

SLEEVES

Cast on 49 (51, 55) sts and, beg with a knit row (RS), work 2 rows St st.

Next row (pattern set-up row): k4 (5, 7) *yfwd, k2tog, k8. Rep from * to last 5 (6, 8) sts then yfwd, k2tog, k3 (4, 6). Work straight in ladder st patt until sleeve measures 10¼ (9½, 10¼) inches.

Inc 1 st at each end of next row and every foll 6th (7th, 6th) row until 59 (61, 65) sts, then work straight until sleeve measures 17 inches, or length desired.

SHAPE SLEEVE HEAD

Bind off 4 (4, 5) sts at beg of next 2 rows then dec 1 st at both ends of every foll row 5 (4, 1) times. Dec 1 st at both ends of every foll alt row 7 (9, 12) times and then every row 5 (5, 3) times. Bind off rem 17 (19, 23) sts loosely.

FINISHING

Carefully block all pieces to size, using a warm steam iron on WS, held above work to avoid flattening fabric. Neatly join shoulder seams. Set in sleeves, easing to fit where necessary. Working from the RS, join side and sleeve seams using mattress stitch, working 1 st in from side edge, and leaving lower 2 inches of sleeve seam open.

TRIM

Beg at side seam, and working from RS, crochet the 2-row picot trim (as per instructions for top) around all edges of jacket, ending at the same side seam. Beg at start of sleeve seam 2 inches above lower edge of sleeve), work trim along the short exposed unseamed edge and around lower sleeve, ending at seam again.

Give the trim a final light press.

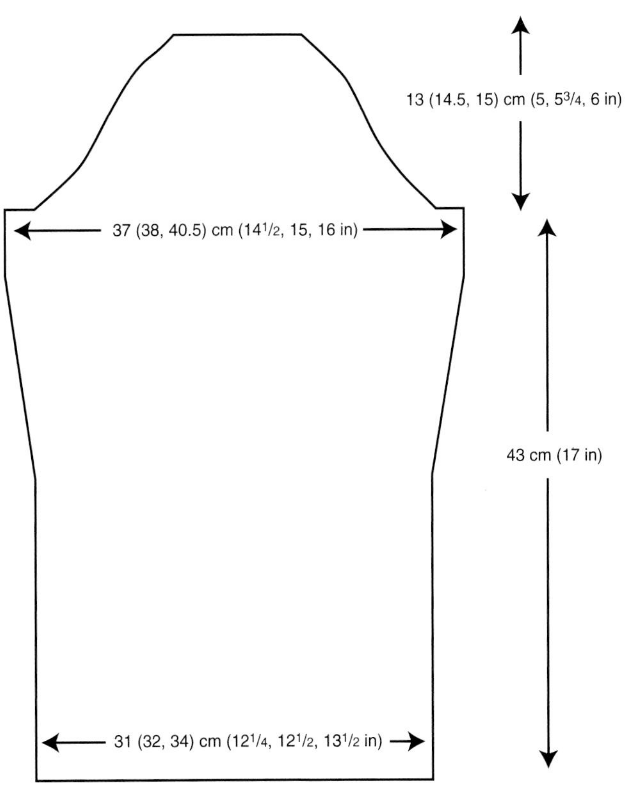

Schematic – Jacket Sleve

Chunky cable and check rug

Richly patterned knitted rugs make gorgeous heirlooms, but not everyone has the time, skill or patience to devote to them. This contemporary version knits up quickly in a chunky mohair-mix yarn on large needles. It features vertical panels of alternating moss-stitch and stockinette squares. Each panel of three squares is separated from the next by cables; these twist first to the right then to the left, making the design symmetrical.

The pattern is given in chart form; if you have never worked with charts before, see the explanation on page 28.

Materials

Nine 3½ ounce balls Cleckheaton Gusto 10, Col 2095 Blue

Tools

Size 13 circular needles, at least 32 inches long

Wool needle

Size

Approx 35½ x 53 inches

Gauge

8½ sts and 10 rows to 4 inches over St st using size 13 needles

Abbreviations and explanations

C4B: make 4-stitch cable: slip 2 sts onto cable needle, hold cable needle at back of work, k2 from left needle, k2 from cable needle (to produce right-twisting cable)

C4F: make 4-stitch cable: slip 2 sts onto cable needle, hold cable needle at front of work, k2 from left needle, k2 from cable needle (to produce left-twisting cable)

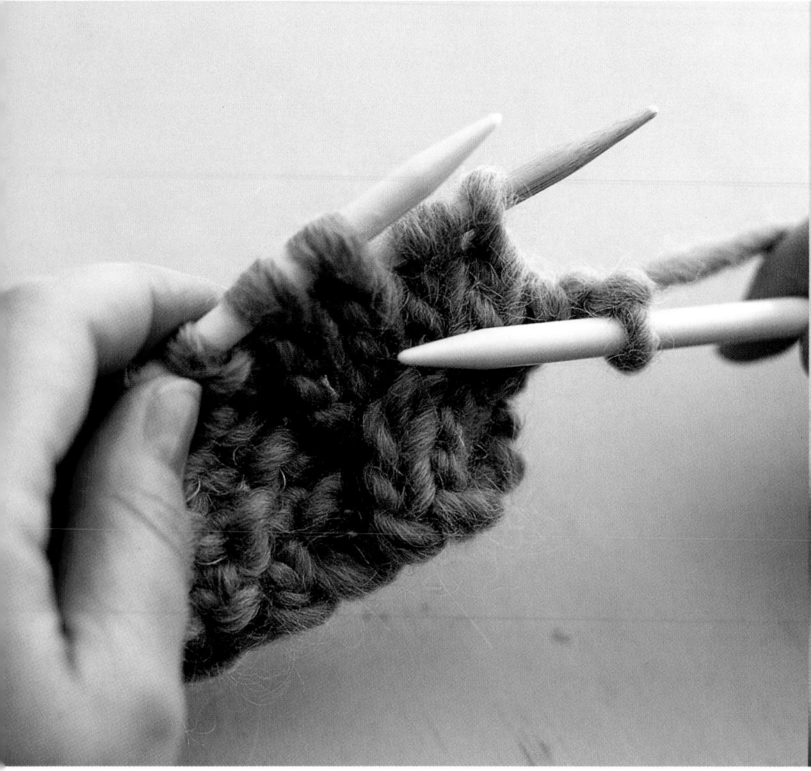

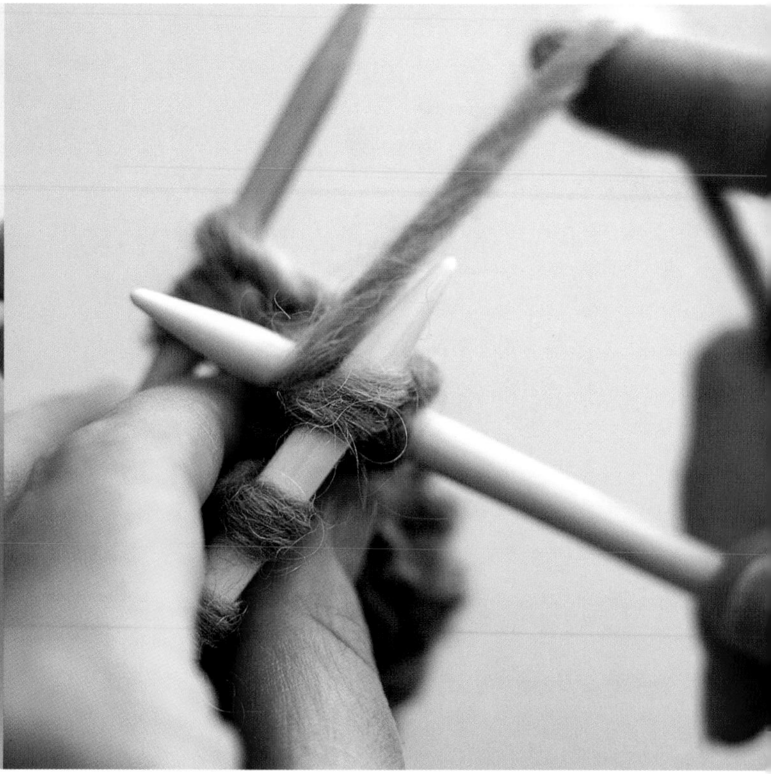

working cable, step 1 For a right-slanting cable (the first and third cables in the design), slip two stitches onto a cable needle and hold at the back of the work.

working cable, step 2 Work the two stitches off the left needle.

KEY ☐ Knit on RS rows, purl on WS rows ⊟ Purl on RS rows, knit on WS rows Front Cable – over 4 sts Back Cable – over 4 sts

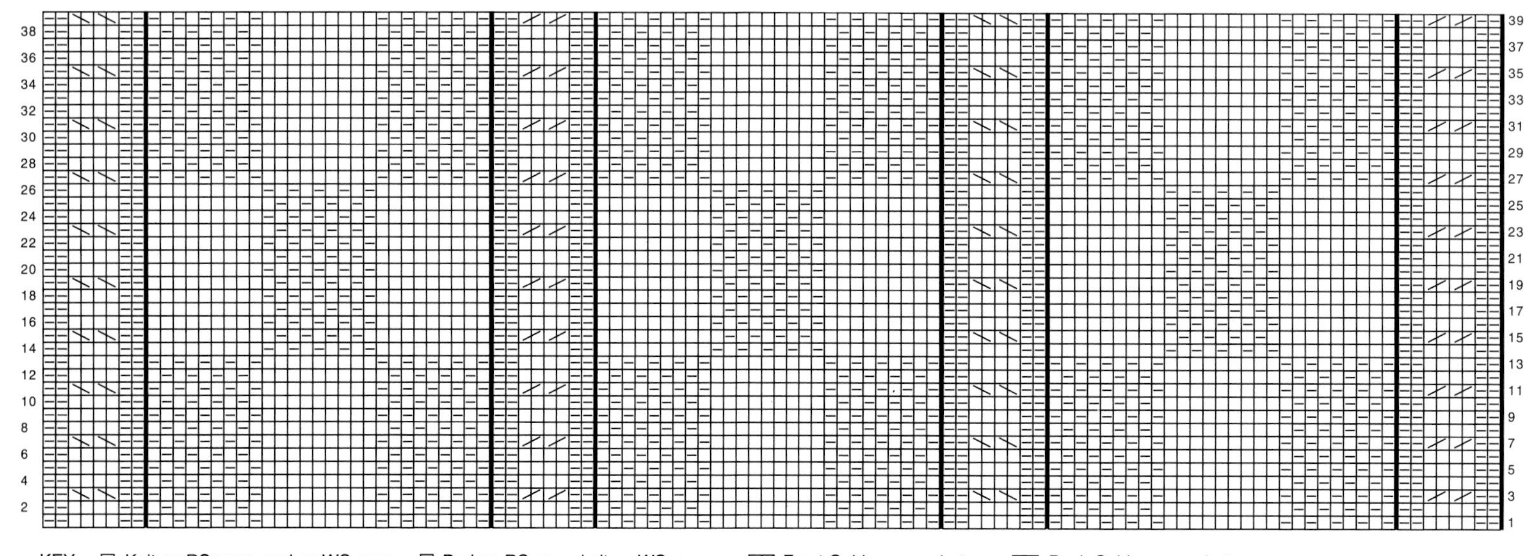

working cable, step 3 Work the two stitches off the cable needle.

left-twisting cable For the second and fourth cables in this design, the cable needle is held at the front of the work, thus changing the direction of the cable's twist.

CO 113 sts, then follow the chart opposite. Work each odd-numbered row as a RS row, reading the chart from right to left; work each even-numbered row as a WS row, reading the chart from left to right.

When following the chart, think of the rug as being constructed in panels; each cable (along with the 2 purl sts on either side) forms one panel, and the three squares of alternating moss stitch and stockinette form another panel. Once the design is set up, it will be fairly easy to follow by sight, but keep a record of the number of rows you have made so that you know when to start alternating the squares vertically.

After Row 39 of chart, cont in patt. Exact vertical pattern repeats cannot be given for the overall design, as the cables are worked over a different number of rows from the textured squares; the cables are turned on the 3rd and foll 4th rows and the squares of moss stitch and stockinette are worked over 9 sts and 13 rows.

Cont in patt until the rug is 9 squares long, ending on Row 38 (a WS row). For the next (RS) row, bind off loosely in patt.

To finish, sew in ends.

Hints

This rug is unsuitable for babies, as the short fibers of the mohair component shed readily; the rug is also very heavy, and could potentially cause the baby to overheat.

Felted bag and hat

The fibers of untreated wool have a natural tendency to shrink and mat when washed incorrectly or rubbed. Normally you wouldn't want to encourage this, but this trait can be exploited to produce lovely felted fabrics and garments such as this hat and bag. The items are knitted first, then machine-washed in hot water; the agitation of the wash cycle combined with the hot water causes the wool to shrink and felt. You can easily do this at home, but you need to keep an eye on the items so that they don't shrink beyond the required size. It's a good idea to knit a small swatch and then wash it as instructed so that you can check the shrinkage rate and see how long it takes to felt.

Materials for bag

10½ ounces of DK wool in each of lime green for Main Color (MC) and marine blue for Contrast Color (CC)

Tools

Size 10½ circular needles, 24 or 32 inches long

Size 10½ double-pointed needles (or sizes required to give correct gauge)

Wool needle

Large button or toggle

Size

Body of bag: width 13½ inches at base, 21 inches at top; height of sides 9½ inches.

Straps: 32 inches long

Gauge

13 sts and 17 rows to 4 inches over St st using size 10½ needles and two strands of wool held together

Felted bag

A double strand of DK wool is used throughout. The finished knitted bag is large and loose but the felting process will result in a firm fabric. Garter st is used for the base. Stockinette is used for the body of the bag. The straps and button loop are knitted separately. The sides of the bag are knitted with the wrong side (WS) facing, so the purl side is the right side (RS). The bag is turned inside out and the top border, straps and button loop are all sewn into place before the bag is felted. The button is added after felting.

BASE OF BAG

With circular needles and 2 strands of CC held together, CO 48 sts.
Knit 48 rows.
Leaving sts on the needle, rotate work and pick up and k 24 sts (1 st for each ridge) on the side edge, 48 sts from the cast-on edge and 24 sts from the other short side [144 sts]. Place a marker at beg of round.
Change to MC and cont knitting with circular needles until yarn is almost finished, ending at start of round where marker was placed.
To make top border, change to CC and cont for a further 4 inches.
Bind off loosely. Cut yarn, leaving approx 3 m (3 yd) for sewing top border. Fold the top border in half to the inside of bag (RS) and slip-stitch the bound-off edge to bag.

STRAPS

Using 2 strands of CC and dpns, CO 2 sts.
Rows 1 & 3 Knit.
Row 2 Inc in each st [4 sts].
Row 4 Inc in 1st st, k to last st, inc in last st [6 sts].
Row 5 & 6 Rep rows 3 and 4 [8 sts].
Knit 5 more rows without further inc. Do not turn work after last row.
Begin making knitted cord (as explained on page 37) for strap: slide stitches to other end of needle, take yarn across back of work, and keeping a firm gauge on the yarn, k8. Do not turn work, but continue in this manner until work measures 39½ inches from cast-on.
Turn work and k 5 rows.
Now start the dec for the last 6 rows.
6th-last row k2tog, k to last 2 st, k2tog [6 sts].
5th-last row Knit.
4th-last & 3rd-last rows Rep last 2 rows (4 sts).
2nd-last row k2tog, k2tog [2 sts].
Bind off last 2 sts.

BUTTON LOOP

Using 2 strands of CC, CO 35 sts.
Next row Bind off 35 sts.

FINISHING

With RS facing, pin straps to outside of bag on both sides, taking care that they are placed evenly. Measure distance between the handles of one side and pin the button loop in the middle of this space. Slip-stitch the straps and button loop securely onto the bag. Sew in any loose ends.

FELTING THE BAG

Place the bag in a zippered mesh laundry bag or a pillowcase tied at the neck. Half fill a top-loading washing machine with hot water and add a generous amount of wool-approved detergent. The water level

Joining yarns by splicing

When joining yarn that has not been treated to make it machine-washable, you can splice the ends together. Splicing exploits the tendency of untreated wool to mat and felt. To splice, unravel one end of the wool and tear off about 3 inches of one strand of the wool. Do the same to the yarn to be joined. Wet both ends with warm water and overlap them on the palm of your hand. Rub very vigorously to create heat, while also moving the join up and down your palm until both ends have felted together.

For other yarns, you will need to tie the ends together using a reef knot (see diagram on page 49). Where possible, make the knot at the side of the work, not in the middle of a row. Using a wool needle, weave the tails of the knot along the seams or edges of the work.

should be high enough to allow the bag free movement during the felting process.

Start the machine and check the bag every few minutes. You may need to wash the bag 2 or 3 times before it reaches the desired size. Start the wash again before the machine finishes its cycle and begins to empty the water.

Once the bag has felted to a firm fabric, remove the bag and rinse it in warm water. Spin the rinse water out on a gentle spin cycle. Stretch the bag and the straps into shape and allow to dry in the shade. Once dry, sew button to center of bag on opposite side to loop.

To care for your bag, gently hand-wash, reshape and dry in the shade. Use a warm iron if you wish.

Felted broad-brimmed hat

Using size 10½ straight needles and mohair and wool in MC held together, CO 91 sts. Work 2 rows in garter st.

Row 3 (k8, inc in next st), rep to end.

Row 4 (k9, inc in next st), rep to end [110 sts].

Row 5 to 14 Cont in garter st.

Row 15 (k9, k2tog), rep to end.

Row 16 (k8, k2tog), rep to end.

Row 17 (k7, k2tog), rep to end.

Row 18 (k6, k2tog), rep to end.

Change to size 10½ circular needles and CC. Cont with circular needles until work measures 8 inches from where you began knitting with the circular needles.

SHAPE CROWN

Change to MC. Place marker at beg of row.

Row 1 (k5, k2tog), rep to end of round.

Row 2 Knit.

Row 3 (k5, k2tog), rep to end of round.

Row 4 Knit.

Row 5 (k2, k2tog), rep to end of round.

Row 6 Knit.

Row 7 (k1, k2tog), rep to end of round.

Row 8 (k2 tog), rep until 4 sts rem.

Cut yarn and sew through rem sts to secure. Using a flat seam, sew up bottom seam on the garter st brim and darn in any loose ends. Your hat is now ready to felt.

FELTING

Put a top-loading washing machine on the small load setting and fill it with hot water. Add a generous amount of wool-approved detergent. Set the machine on a normal cycle, keeping watch and checking the hat frequently. You may need to stop the machine and start a second or third cycle to achieve the desired effect. Keeping watch on the felting process will ensure the hat felts to the required size. (It's very easy to end up with a doll-sized hat.)

When the hat is sufficiently felted, rinse it in warm water, spin out the excess rinse water and place the hat onto a hat block or wig stand. Allow to dry in the shade.

CARE

Using wool-approved detergent, gently hand-wash and rinse in warm water. Spin out the rinse water on spin cycle in washing machine. Reshape, place on a hat block or wig stand (an upturned bowl will also do the trick) and dry in the shade.

Materials for hat

Main Color (MC): 1¾ ounces DK mohair in lime green; 1¾ ounces DK wool in lime green

Contrast Color (CC): 1¾ ounces DK mohair in marine blue; 1¾ ounces DK wool in marine blue)

Tools

Size 10½ needles

Size 10½ circular needles, 16 inches long

(or sizes required to give correct gauge)

Hat block or wig stand

Size

To fit average-sized woman's head (approx 56 cm/22 in)

Gauge

12 sts and 18 rows to 4 inches over St st on size 10½ needles using wool and mohair yarns held together

Snake-cable belt

snake cable The design is worked over 8 rows.

finishing Fasten the button through one of the holes in the knitted fabric.

This snake cable gives a braided effect. It looks intricate but is surprisingly easy and rhythmic to knit.

Materials

One 3½ oz skein Noro Iro, Col 47

Tools

Size 9 needles

1 large oval button

Size

2¾ inches wide

Gauge

12 sts and 18 rows to 4 inches over St st on size 9 needles

CO 18 sts.

Row 1 Knit.

Row 2 Purl.

Row 3 (C6B) 3 times.

Row 4 Purl.

Row 5 Knit.

Row 6 Purl.

Row 7 k3, (C6F) twice, k3.

Row 8 Purl.

These 8 rows form patt.

Cont in patt until work is desired length plus approx 2⅓–3¼ inches for overlap, ending with Row 8.

Bind off. Sew in loose ends.

Using strong thread, sew the button in the center of one end of the belt, approx 2 inches in from the end. Fasten the button through one of the central gaps in the other end of the belt made by the cable patt (between rows 7 and 8). Alternatively, you could fasten the belt with a large brooch or kilt pin.

This design can be made wider if desired; the snake-cable pattern will work over any multiple of 6 sts.

Fine lace shawl vest

This shawl–vest hybrid is made of two strips of easy lace joined down the center with two holes left for the arms. A lace border is then added. Like most lace items, this project must be blocked; when taken straight off the needles, it is crumpled and the lace stitches indistinct. Once correctly blocked, as explained on pages 22 and 104–5, the lace pattern opens up beautifully.

Materials

3 ounces Artisan NZ Merino Lace Weight (each of the two pieces takes just under 1½ ounces of yarn)

Tools

Size 3 needles
Size 5 needles
Extra-long knitting needles for blocking
Rustless pins
Safety pins
Sewing needle and polyester thread

Size

After blocking: approx 65 x 30 inches, including border

Gauge

Before blocking: 20 sts and 30 rows to 4 inches over patt, using size 3 needles
After blocking: 16 sts and 22 rows to 4 inches over patt, using size 3 needles

Abbreviations and explanations

k: Knit
k2tog: Knit 2 stitches together
K2Tog: Knit 2 stitches together where first stitch is the last stitch of the border pattern and second stitch is from the shawl
p2tog: Purl 2 stitches together
sPf: Slip stitch purlwise with yarn in front, then bring yarn to back ready to knit
yf: Yarn forward (bring yarn to front of work)
yrn (yarn round needle): This makes a loop over the right-hand needle when working purl stitches. The purl stitch is worked with the yarn at the front of the work, rather than at the back as is usual. Wind yarn from the front over the right-hand needle and back to the front, ready to work the purl 2 together

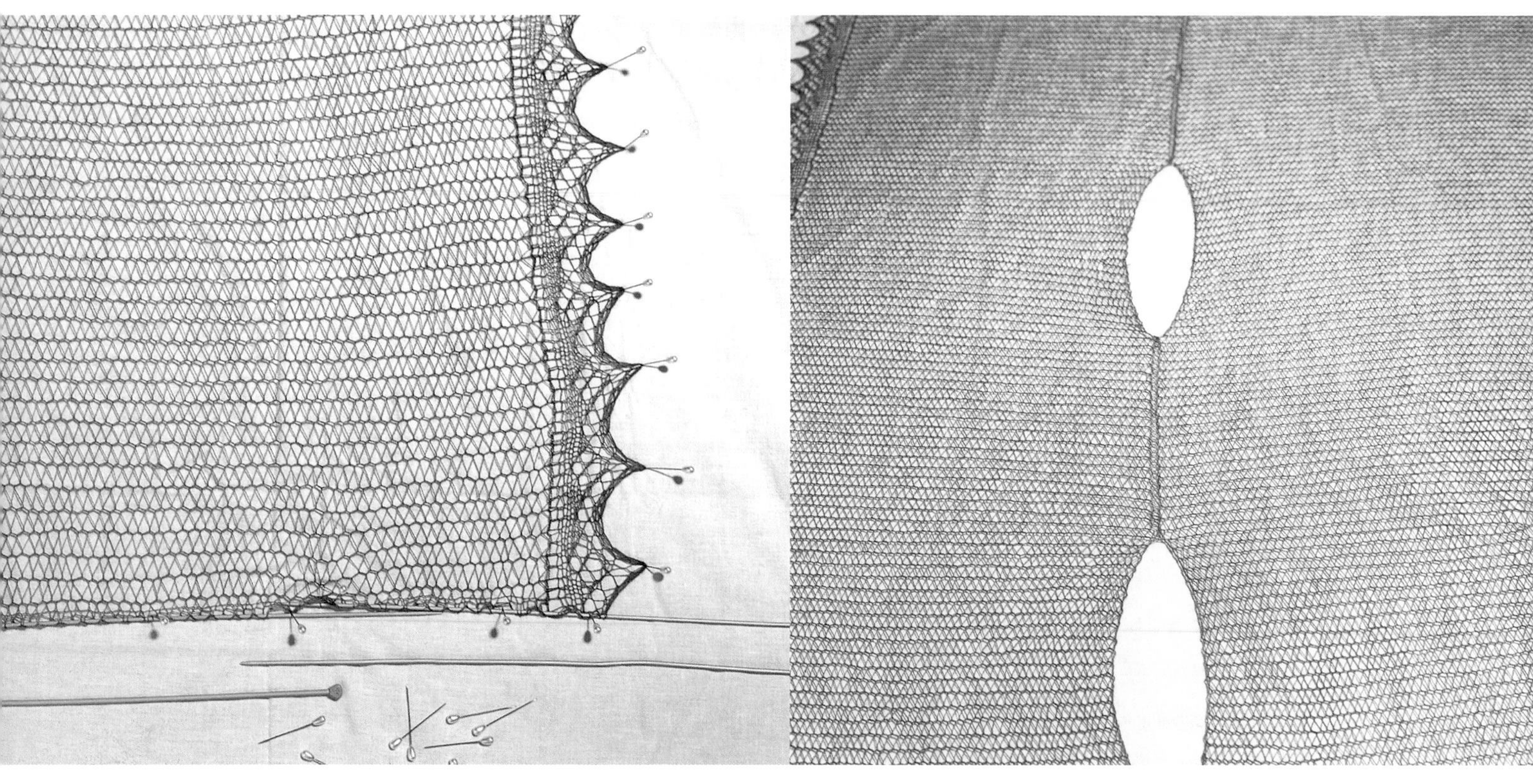

blocking Pin out damp garment to measurements, using long knitting needles threaded through the ends of the pieces then pinned into place.

opening armholes Once the blocked garment is dry, pull out the armhole threads to open up the armholes.

Hints

Form the p2tog very carefully. Make sure the two stitches (the stitch and the loop formed by the yrn) are both slipped off the left-hand needle. The p2tog is always the stitch and the yrn is always the loop. If you find you have a loop left before the next p2tog, lift this loop over the stitch behind it on the left-hand needle.

Alternatively, the shawl can be worked in garter stitch (knit every row) on size 5 needles.

SHAWL VEST

Make 2 pieces the same.

Using size 3 needles, CO 272 sts, leaving a 16 inch tail to use for sewing later.

Work every row thus: p2, *yrn, p2tog; rep from * to last 2 sts, p2tog.

When work measures 10 inches slightly stretched, or there is ½ ounce yarn left, whichever comes first, change to size 5 needles and work 1 row thus: p2, * yrn, p2tog; rep from * to last 2 sts, yrn, p2 [273 sts].

Do not break yarn. Cast on 7 sts and using size 5 needles, work lace border as given in graphs and instructions opposite. Bind off loosely. Weave in end of cast-off yarn.

FINISHING

Lay the 2 pieces flat, placing cast-on edges together. Mark off the measurements for joining seams (see Diagram 1) and sew together as invisibly as possible. Weave in the ends of the thread back along the sewn seam to finish off. Using polyester sewing thread, sew the armholes together, leaving a 6 inch tail at either end. Do not secure this sewing; it will be pulled out after blocking to open up the armholes.

BLOCKING

Soak the garment in warm water for 30 minutes. Gently squeeze out excess water and roll up in a clean, colorfast towel to absorb water. Place a clean sheet on a carpeted floor or on a bed.

Thread straight knitting needles through the ends of the garment, overlapping as necessary. Pin out the needles, stretching the work to the finished size. Pin out each lace point, stretching as you go. Keep adjusting the pins to keep the garment straight and stretched. The stretch should be comfortably firm.

Rub your hands gently over the stretched surface. This tangles the small fibers of the wool and helps to hold the pattern in place. Allow to dry completely. Remove the knitting needles and pins, then pull out the armhole threads.

BORDER PATTERN

Cast on 7 sts.

Set-up Row 1 sPf, k2, yf, k3, K2Tog (last st from border and the first st from shawl).

Set-up Row 2 Knit (see Diagram 2 for chart of cast-on and set-up rows).

Begin border pattern (see Diagram 3):

Row 1 sPf, k2, yf, k4, K2Tog.

Row 2 Knit.

Row 3 sPf, k2, yf, k5, K2Tog.

Row 4 Knit.

Row 5 sPf, k2, yf, k2, yf, k2tog, k2, K2Tog.

Row 6 Knit.

Row 7 sPf, k2, yf, k2, [yf, k2tog twice], k1, K2Tog.

Row 8 Knit.

Row 9 sPf, k3, yf, k2tog, k1, yf, k2tog, k2, K2Tog.

Row 10 k10, k2tog.

Row 11 sPf, k3, yf, k2tog, k4, K2Tog.

Row 12 k9, k2tog.

Row 13 sPf, k3, yf, k2tog, k3, K2Tog.

Row 14 k8, k2tog.

Row 15 sPf, k3, yf, k2tog, k2, K2Tog.

Row 16 k7, k2tog.

These last 16 rows form patt. Rep these 16 rows until all the shawl sts have been used up. Bind off and weave in thread.

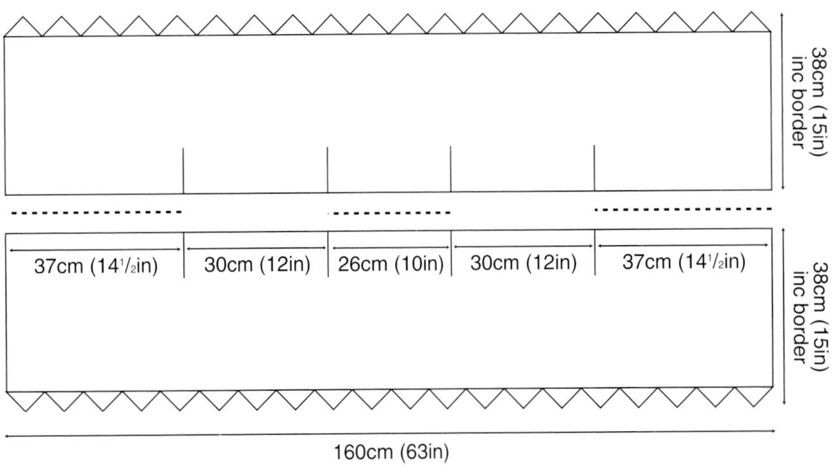

diagram 1 Sew up as shown.

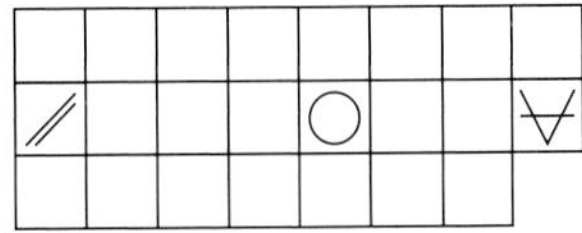

diagram 2 Setting up the stitches for the border pattern: first row is cast-on row, second row is set-up row 1, third row is set-up row 2

Chart Symbols

Slip stitch purlwise with yarn in front, then bring yarn to back ready to knit

Yarn forward

k2tog

K2Tog where first stitch is the last stitch of the lace border pattern and second stitch is the stitch from the shawl

Knit

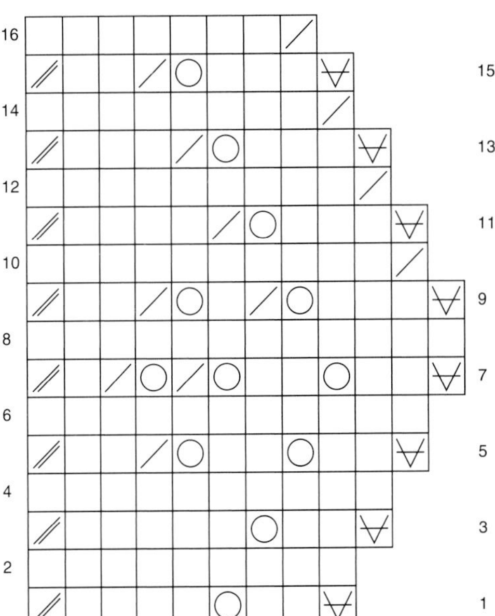

diagram 3 Chart for lace edging; once set-up rows have been established, these 16 rows form patt.

Beaded jewelry

The technique of incorporating beads into the structure of knitted cloth is hundreds of years old, and dates back to the early traditions of knitting. The basic principle of bead knitting is very simple, but the technique can sometimes take a little time to perfect. Use a variety of sizes so the beads will fit together like a random jigsaw puzzle. Use a yarn appropriate to the size of the beads; small beads will not work with thick yarn. Fine yarn such as beading thread or buttonhole thread is excellent. Most buttonhole thread will knit on size 2–3 needles and is available in a range of colors. Some manufacturers make linen and lurex threads, which can be fun to use.

Jewelry findings such as earring hooks, lobster clasps, crimps, jump rings, and brooch clasps are available in various sizes and finishes from most craft suppliers or beading stores.

Materials for Pendant

108 glass beads in assorted sizes
Buttonhole thread
1 lobster clasp
4 crimps
2 closed jump rings

Tools for Pendant

Size 2–3 needles
Crimping pliers
Darning needle

Materials for Brooch

102 glass beads of assorted sizes
Buttonhole thread
1 bar-style brooch pin, 1 inch long

Tools for Brooch

Size 2–3 needles
Darning needle

Materials for Earrings

48 glass beads of assorted sizes (choose even numbers of each bead, so that the earrings will be identical)
1 set earring hooks
Buttonhole thread

Tools for earrings

Size 2–3 needles
Darning needle

Size

Earrings approx 1½ inches long
Brooch approx 2½ inches long
Necklace approx 10½ inches long

Gauge

Gauge is not critical for these items

Pendant

Thread 48 beads onto the yarn. CO 5 sts.
Row 1 Knit.
Row 2 Slip first stitch, place 1 bead against knitting and k second st, k third st, place 1 bead against knitting and k fourth st, k fifth st.
Row 3 As for Row 2.
Row 4 Slip first st, k second st, place 1 bead against knitting and k third stitch, k fourth st, place 1 bead against knitting and k fifth st.
Row 5 As for Row 4.
Repeat Rows 2–5 until all beads have been incorporated.
Bind off, leaving a 6 inch tail. Stitch the tails of the yarn into the fabric of the pendant to conceal them and cut them off close to the knitted fabric.

Cut a piece of yarn approx 3 feet long and double it over. Feed the folded end into the needle and pass it through the fabric at the top of the pendant. You should have a small loop on one side and two ends of yarn on the other. Pull the ends of yarn through the loop and pull tight. Thread one large bead on one end of yarn and two small beads on the other, then push them down towards the pendant, securing them loosely in place with a knot. Rep until you have incorporated 10 medium or large beads and 20 small beads, and tied 10 knots (approx ½ inch apart). Thread two crimps onto the yarn, followed by a jump ring. Thread the yarn back through the crimps and pull the yarn through to give the desired length from the pendant (8¼ inches will give a classic 17 inch necklace).

Then, using the crimping pliers, squeeze the crimps flat (not too tightly, or you will cut the yarn). Trim off the ends.
Repeat the process with the remaining beads to create the other side of the necklace, up to the point where you have incorporated the remaining beads and have tied 10 knots. Thread two crimps onto the yarn, followed by a jump ring and a lobster clasp. Thread yarn back through the crimps and pull yarn through to give the same length as the other side of the pendant. Squeeze crimps flat and trim ends of yarn.

Brooch

Thread 102 beads onto the yarn, alternating sizes. CO 13 sts.
Row 1 Knit.
Row 2 Slip first stitch, (place bead against knitting and k 1 st, k next st) to end.
Row 3 Knit.
Row 4 Slip 1 st, (k 1 st, place bead against knitting and k next st) to end.
Row 5 Knit.
Repeat Rows 2–5 until all 102 beads are incorporated.
Knit 6 more rows.
Bind off in single rib. Cut off the yarn, leaving a 9 inch tail. Use this tail of yarn to stitch the flat (cast-off) end of the brooch fabric around the bar of the brooch pin (this will become the top of the brooch). Secure it tightly through the holes in the bar so that it will not slide around. When the pin is secure, trim off the end of the yarn. Stitch the tail of yarn at the lower (cast-on) edge into the fabric of the brooch to conceal it and cut off the end close to the knitting.

Earrings

Make 2 the same.
Divide the beads into 2 piles, splitting different beads evenly between the piles to give matching earrings.
For the first earring, thread 1 pile of 24 beads onto the yarn, alternating sizes; thread the larger ones first, so they end up at the bottom of the earring, then medium, and finally small beads.
CO 4 sts, leaving a 6 inch tail.
Row 1 Knit.
Row 2 Slip the first st from the left needle onto the right needle without knitting it. Draw up 1 bead, place it against the knitting and k the second st. K the third st, then place 1 bead against the knitting and k the fourth st.
Row 3 As for Row 2.
Row 4 Slip first st, k second st, place bead against knitting and k third st, k fourth st.
Row 5 As for Row 4.
Repeat rows 2–5 until all 24 beads have been used.
Bind off, then cut yarn, leaving a tail of about 9 inches. Thread this tail of yarn into the darning needle and stitch it firmly through the bottom of the earring hook. Then darn the remaining yarn into the fabric of the earring and cut off the end close to the earring.
Take the bottom tail of yarn (at the cast-on edge) and stitch it into the fabric of the earring to conceal it, then cut off the end close to the earring.

earring This shows the bound-off end attached to the earring hook

back of brooch This shows the brooch pin attached to the flat (bound-off) end of the knitted fabric

Index

THUNDER BAY
P·R·E·S·S

Thunder Bay Press
An imprint of the Advantage Publishers Group
5880 Oberlin Drive, San Diego, CA 92121-4794
www.thunderbaybooks.com

All notations of errors or omissions should be sent to Thunder Bay Press, Editorial Department, at the above address. All other correspondence (author inquiries, permissions, and rights) concerning the content of this book should be addressed to Murdoch Books Pty Limited, Pier 8/9, 23 Hickson Road, Millers Point NSW 2000, Australia.

ISBN-13: 978-1-59223-693-0
ISBN-10: 1-59223-693-6

Library of Congress Cataloging-in-Publication data available upon request

Chief Executive: Juliet Rogers
Publisher: Kay Scarlett
Design concept: Tracy Loughlin
Art direction: Vivien Valk
Designer: Jacqueline Richards
Project manager and editor: Janine Flew
Photographer: Natasha Milne
Stylist: Sarah O'Brien
Charts and diagrams: Amanda McKittrick, Heather Menzies, Jacqueline Richards
Production: Monika Paratore
Project designers and makers: Diana Crossing/Minx Handknits (Snowflake slippers); Amanda Ducker/Minx Handknits (Men's sweater, Hot-water bottle cover, Multicolored beret); Sarah Durrant (Pure silk top, Tie-front jacket); Janine Flew (Casual bag, Two-toned ruched scarf, Triangular garter-stitch shawl, Loop-stitch cushion, Braided chunky velvet scarf, Clutch purse, Chunky cable and check rug, Snake-cable belt); Liz Gemmell (Simple gelatin-dyed lace scarf, Fine lace shawl vest); Amanda McKittrick (Tea cozy); Stephanie J. Milne (Beaded jewelry); Jane Slicer-Smith (Two-toned jacket, Miter throw); Nancy Tyack/Minx Handknits (Tassel hat); Nicola Wilkins (Garter-stitch mohair cushion, Double-rib mohair throw, Felted bag, Felted broad-brimmed hat)

Printed in China by 1010 Printing International Limited
1 2 3 4 5 10 09 08 07 06

The Publisher and project designers wish to thank Audrey Armstrong, Michelle Cutler, Elvie Dascombe, Diana Grivas, Elsie Langford, Shirley Honeyman, and Ros Waters for knitting and pattern testing.